STUDY OF RECRUITMENT STRATEGY WITH REFERENCE TO EMPLOYEE RETENTION IN INDIAN BANKING AND INSURANCE SECTOR

SUBMITTED TO
SVKM's NMIMS UNIVERSITY

SUBMITTED FOR
DEGREE OF Ph.D. (MANAGEMENT STUDIES)

SUBMITTED BY
SWATI AMIT VISPUTE

UNDER THE GUIDANCE OF
THESIS ADVISORY COMMITTEE

DR. M. N. WELLING, CHAIRPERSON
PRO-VICE CHANCELLOR, NMIMS UNIVERSITY

DR. VIDYA NAIK, MEMBER
DEAN, NGA-SCE, NMIMS UNIVERSITY

MR. SUNIT MEHRA, MEMBER
MANAGING PARTNER, HUNT PARTNERS

SCHOOL OF BUSINESS MANAGEMENT
JUNE 2014

© Copyright (2014) Swati A. Vispute

Declaration

I hereby declare that the research work embodied in the present thesis entitled **"Study of Recruitment Strategy with Reference to Employee Retention in Indian Banking and Insurance Sector"** is the outcome of my own efforts except for the guidance received from my Research Guide and the references to the earlier works that have been duly acknowledged.

I further declare that this work has not been submitted to this University or any other university for any other exam.

Place: Mumbai　　　　　　　　　(Signature of Research Student)

Date:　　　　　　　　　　　　　　Swati Amit Vispute

Certificate

Name of the Guide: Dr. M. N. Welling

Address: NMIMS University
V. L. Mehta Road, Vile Parle (W)
Mumbai 400 056

This is to certify that the Thesis entitled **"Study of Recruitment Strategy with Reference to employee Retention in Indian Banking and Insurance Sector"** embodies the work of the candidate himself / herself. The candidate has worked under my guidance and in my opinion the Thesis fulfills the requirements of SVKM's NMIMS University, Mumbai relating to Degree of Ph. D. (Management Studies).

Place: Mumbai   (Signature of the Guide)
Date: Dr. M. N. Welling
                Chairperson, Thesis Advisory Committee

Acknowledgement

As I see to this end of a very momentous journey, I thank Heavenly Grace, for giving me strength and patience to endure successfully my quest to complete this thesis. I sincerely thank all those people who made this thesis possible and an unforgettable experience for me.

I would like to express my heartfelt gratitude to my Thesis Advisory Committee Chair, Dr. M. N. Welling. I have been amazingly fortunate to have an advisor who gave me the freedom to explore on my own and at the same time the guidance to recover when my steps faltered. I thank him for bestowing his confidence, his encouragement in me through his wise counsel throughout the process. My second Thesis Advisory Committee member Dr. Vidya Naik has been always there to listen and give advice. During the times of ups and downs, her words helped me in keeping myself on track. A thousand thanks to you Ma'am! I am also grateful to Mr. Sunit Mehra; Thesis Advisory Committee member who helped me with his valued and experienced inputs on industry perspective of research. His knowledge and expertise were of a great help in setting up the study.

I sincerely acknowledge the hard work put in by the experts who reviewed my research proposal, synopsis, and thesis. Due to their comments, I could improve on my study.

I appreciate All India Council for Technical Education (AICTE) for conferring National Doctoral Fellowship (NDF) on me. Their financial assistance was of great support to me. I am also grateful to Human Capital for Third Sector for supporting me financially for my international conference.

My sincere thanks go to various departments at NMIMS University, especially library staff for their consistent help during my study. I am also thankful to Mumbai University, Tata Institute of Social Sciences, Indian School of Business, Indian Institute of Management –Ahmedabad, and University of Nevada, for allowing me to visit their library and use library resources.

My sincere thanks go to all Human Resources Head and Recruitment heads of banks and insurance companies who participated in this research project with interest and enthusiasm. I would like to thank to Mr. Gautam Chainani (Former CPO, Birla Sunlife), and Mr. Suresh Mani (Birla Sunlife) for their valuable inputs during the study.

A special thanks to my family for their love and encouragement. Words cannot express how much I owe to my parents Shri. Baburao D. Pawar and Smt. Shakuntala B. Pawar, for giving me support to reach for my educational dreams. I dedicate this thesis to my parents. I am grateful to God for giving me caring brothers, Pravin dada and Amit. I deeply appreciate their unconditional belief in me. I am thankful to my in-laws, Shri Dilip Vispute and Smt. Leelavati Vispute for their blessings in this journey. Last, but very important person in my life, my husband; Amit: a whole hearted thank you for your enormous support and your supportive companionship. It's all because of you I could work persistently on this thesis. Thank you for standing by my side all the time when I was looking down the barrel.

Abstract

In India, there is an acute shortage of banking and insurance talent in the marketplace as there is no formal banking and insurance education. Therefore, it becomes essential to retain the existing talent. Before an organization thinks about retaining employees it is essential to have in place a strategy that attracts the right people. Thus, effective recruitment is the first step to retain staff.

This study aims to present findings of study of recruitment strategy adopted by the banks and insurance companies in India and retention of employees in the same organizations. Specifically, the objective of this study is to find the relationship between elements of recruitment strategy and categories of employees retained. Based on previous literature and in-depth interviews with HR and recruitment heads of banks and insurance companies, a survey was designed and distributed to banks and insurance professionals across India.

The results of this study are supportive of the existence of significant relationships between the set of independent variables and employee retention. It is evident from this study that recruitment strategy variables individually show significant correlation with post-hire outcomes of retention like commitment, burnout, and turnover intent.

The companies should pay attention not only to evaluating formal qualifications, job relevant technical ability, etc., but also share right information at right time, give positive recruitment experience, fair interview structure, and execute realistic applicant attractors.

Providing a realistic picture of the role and work profile, potential future career opportunities, working conditions, brief information about co-workers, and level of responsibility in the organization as well as training and development opportunities, will help employees make fully informed choices and develop commitment as also minimize attrition among them.

The study reveals that creating personable, competent recruitment process with clear pre-visit information will help organization to influence commitment of employees, their feeling of burnout, and intention to leave the organization.

Similarly, structured interviews that consider topics discussed during interview, information possessed by the interviewer, interviewer's willingness to listen to the interviewees, his/her ability to control interview, knowledge of the content of the application form, and giving opportunity to applicant for an effective self-presentation plays an important role in influencing commitment of employees.

When applicant attractors are extensively used by the organization in recruiting employees and later fulfilled those factors, it helps organization to influence employee commitment in a positive manner. But, if the same is not fulfilled it leads to intention of turnover among employees.

This study has important implications for both practitioners and future researchers. Future researchers can replicate the study to develop recruitment and retention model. Practitioners can improve their recruitment strategy considering its retention effects.

Keywords: Recruitment strategy, employee retention, organizational commitment, turnover intent, burnout

Table of Contents

Declaration iii
Certificate iv
Acknowledgement v
Abstract vii
List of Abbreviations xii
List of Figures xiii
List of Tables xiv

CHAPTER I – INTRODUCTION 1

    1.1 Chapter Overview 1
    1.2 Introduction to Problem 1
    1.3 Need for Research 4
    1.4 Context of the study 7
    1.5 Research Problem 9
    1.6 Objectives of Study 10
    1.7 Scope and Delimitations of the Study 10
    1.8 Significance of study 11

CHAPTER II – REVIEW OF LITERATURE 12

    2.1 Chapter Overview 12
    2.2 Theoretical Foundations 12
        2.2.2 Strategic HRM (SHRM) and HRM Strategy 13
        2.2.3 Recruitment Strategy 19
    2.3 Cost Considerations 27
        2.3.1 Cost of Turnover 28
    2.4 Recruitment Strategy Variables 30
        2.4.1 Information Shared 30
        2.4.2 Recruitment Process Experience 35

    2.4.3 Interview Structure 39
    2.4.4 Applicant Attractors 43
    2.4.5 Source of Recruitment 46
  2.5 Employee Retention Variables 52
    2.5.1 Commitment 56
    2.5.2 Burnout 62
    2.5.3 Turnover Intent 70
  2.6 Summary 77
  2.7 Research Gap 78
  2.8 Hypotheses 80
  2.9 Concept Map 85

CHAPTER III – RESEARCH METHODOLOGY 86

  3.1 Chapter Overview 86
  3.2 Type of Study 86
  3.3 Sampling 87
  3.4 Variables and Operational Definitions 89
    3.4.1 Recruitment strategy –
    Independent Variables 89
    3.4.2 Employee Retention –
    Dependent Variables 92
  3.5 Control Variables 93
  3.6 Tools of Measurement 94
  3.7 Data Collection 94

CHAPTER IV – DATA ANALYSIS, HYPOTHESIS TESTING AND DISCUSSION 96

  4.1 Chapter Overview 96
  4.2 Cronbach Alpha 96
  4.4 Correlation Analysis: 107

4.5 Regression Analysis 108
    4.5.1 Analysis of Regression:
    Dependent Variable - Commitment 109
    4.5.2 Analysis of Regression – Burnout 110
    4.5.3 Analysis of Regression: Turnover Intent 116
4.6 Summary of Regression Analysis
and Hypotheses Testing 117
4.7 Discussion 119

CHAPTER V – CONCLUSION, IMPLICATIONS
AND SUGGESTIONS FOR FURTHER RESEARCH 134
    5.1 Chapter Overview... 134
    5.2 Conclusions... 134
    5.3 Implications 140
    5.4 Suggestions for Further Research 141
BIBLIOGRAPHY 143
Annexure A – Questionnaire... 188

List of Abbreviations

HRD – Human Resource Development

HR – Human Resource

HRM – Human Resource Management

SHRM – Strategic Human Resource Management

SRPT- Strategic Reference Points Theory

ASA -Attraction-Selection-Attrition

RJPs - Realistic Job Previews

AART - Applicant Attribution –Reaction Theory

MBI - Maslach Burnout Inventory

List of Figures

Figure 2.1 – Model of the Link between HRM and Performance..

Figure 2.2 – Organizational Strategy...

Figure 2.3 – Model for Future Recruitment Research ....

Figure 2.4 – Updated Theoretical Model of Applicant Reactions to Selection..

Figure 2.5 – Concept Map ....

List of Tables

Table 3.1 – Measures ....
Table 4.1 – Cronbach Alpha ....
Table 4.2 – Descriptive Statistics...
Table 4.3 – Summary of Statistics by Gender ....
Table 4.4 – Summary of Statistics by Age ....
Table 4.5 – Summary of Statistics by Educational Level............
Table 4.6 – Summary of Statistics by
Current Organization Experience ....
Table 4.7 – Summary of Statistics by Total Experience............
Table 4.8 – Summary of Statistics by Management Level..........
Table 4.9 – Summary of Statistics by Type of Organization ....
Table 4.10 – Correlation Analysis ....
Table 4.11 – Regression Analysis –
    Dependent Variable – Commitment ....
Table 4.12 – Regression Analysis – Dependent
    Variable – Emotional Exhaustion..
Table 4.13 – Regression Analysis – Dependent
    Variable – Personal Accomplishment ....
Table4.14 – Regression Analysis - Dependent Variable -
    Depersonalization..
Table 4.15 – Regression Analysis – Dependent
    Variable – Turnover Intent ....
Table 4.16 – Summary of Regression Analysis ....
Table 4.17 – Summary of Hypothesis Testing ....

CHAPTER I

INTRODUCTION

1.1 Chapter Overview

This chapter introduced need for the study, context of the study. It provides information on research problem studied. The delimitations of the study are also explained in this chapter. The chapter is closed with significance of the study.

1.2 Introduction to Problem

The Indian financial system has changed considerably since the 1990s (Herd, R. *et al.*, 2011). Two decades of economic and financial sector reforms have strengthened the Indian economy and transformed the banks and financial institutions in the country. Insurance sector is blessed with Foreign Direct Investment (FDI) in post liberalization era. This has generated enormous employment opportunities for Indian youths. This has further led to talent crunch in the sector and poaching thereafter. Here comes a need for attention on recruitment and retention practices by insurance companies. In banking business, interest rates have been deregulated and new entrants have been allowed in the sector. New private banks have emerged that are more customer-oriented than the older state-owned banks

(Herd, R. *et al.*, 2011). Now the Human Resource Development (HRD) departments of the banks need to be strengthened in terms of Human Resource (HR) practices, recruitment practices, training needs, and compensation package. The HR practices prevalent among banks should be reoriented to meet the emerging challenges in the banking sector (Satpathy et al., 2011).

India has been repeatedly cited to have an abundant and educated workforce. Indian organizations have technically superior workforces with a competitive approach to problem-solving and who are keen to establish themselves as capable of handling all organizational tasks. However, it is observed that the labour market is tightening. Not only organizations are facing acute problem of talent shortages, but also struggling to find 'right talent' for organizational success. As it is a buyer's market, job seekers acquire more of a decisional role in the recruiting process. Therefore, recruitment these days is taken lot more seriously and given lot more thought than it used to be.

Employee retention is a complex issue facing numerous organizations today (Rice, 2005). Hiring right is a powerful first step in reducing unwanted turnover (Harvard Business Essentials, 2002). Therefore, the focus of organizations now has shifted from 'numbers' to 'quality' and from 'recruitment' to 'retention.' Thus, finding and retaining the best employees is a major investment (Evan & Kaye, 2003; Vault, 2006). The study of ranking non-financial variables affecting managerial decisions was conducted by Low & Siesfield (1998). In this study ability to attract and retain talented people is ranked fifth. The report of Society for Human Resource Management (2001) highlight on the fact that firms devote more funds to staffing activities than any other human resource activity. This shows that effective recruitment practices are very much essential.

Attracting and retaining quality employees is the goal of most organizational recruitment efforts (Kecia and Wise, 1999). Therefore organizations that are able to attract good number of quality applicants and remains more careful in the process of their hiring decisions will increase the effectiveness of their overall recruitment system (Boudreau & Rynes, 1985; Murphy, 1986). With increasing competition for human resources, the ability to attract, develop, and retain high-quality employees is becoming the main concern for the industry.

A lot less recruiting will be required if better employee retention is done (Leder Sam, 1999). The retention process commences before an employee joins an organization. It begins when a representative of the company explains the position to be filled, continues during various stages of recruitment, and is reinforced via new employee orientation. Thus, job description, recruitment, selection and employee orientation stands as the foundation of retention (Dibble, 1999). The outcome of research study by Kass et al., (2001) show that in any given group of hires, two-thirds to three-fourths of the quits occur within first three years of employment. Of these, more than fifty percent occur before the end of the first year alone. Effective human resource management can reduce employee turnover and increase employee commitment and productivity within an organization (Kaliprasad, 2006). Haggerty Deb (2002) in his article spells out five steps to fire proof hiring process in order to successfully locate, hire and retain good employees. He calls this as Positivism which he defines as: People, Organization and Strategy Integrated Together in Vital Enterprise. Hacher (1997) in her article provides advice on the personnel screening and selection. By improving these techniques, she contends, it is possible for the mangers to make quality decisions which will result in employees staying in the organization for longer periods of time.

Out of the plentiful practices, the recruitment practice facilitates the entry of an employee in an organization. Hence considering the significance of this function, the researcher has ventured to investigate the relationship between recruitment practices and employees' retention intentions in the Indian banking and insurance sector. Hypothesis validity would help banks and insurance companies, and similar organizations, through the use of more favourable recruitment practices. It will help to reduce or eliminate the employment of individuals who may intend to leave, or who may turn into burnout mode, or encourage employment of individuals who may turn out to be loyal to the organization.

1.3 Need for Research

In the facet of changing world recruitment needs to be evolved. Corporate Recruiting Report (2011) by staffing.org states that globalization, demographic shifts and technological trends continue to roil the job market. Mueller (1982) contends that human capital theory's assumption is that some employees are more productive than others simply because more resources have been invested into those employees in the very same manner as a machine that has had more resources invested into it is appropriate to be more productive.

Previous research literature in the area of recruitment lacked solid theoretical grounding, leading to misrepresentation of complexity in the recruitment process (Breaugh & Starke, 2000; Rynes, 1991). Therefore, first aim of this research is to get overview of theoretical foundations of recruitment and retention studies.

The level of retention among employees partly depends on the people who are hired, the purpose for which they are hired, and partly on how they are managed (Dibble, 1999, Herman,

1999; Kaye and Jordan-Evans, 1999). Therefore, hiring right people for the right jobs is very crucial. As per Smith (2001) 60 percent of total undesirable turnover is due to bad hiring decisions on part of the employer. The aim of majority of the recruitment research studies is estimating the predictive value of recruitment tools; a similar issue is to understand how applicants perceive and react to the recruitment process. In looking for the potential candidates, companies must goad for the traditional employee search. With the wrong choice, morale with other employees can go down. With the right choice it is just as likely to go up (Gage, 2005). It is not possible to rectify the poor decision just by removing the candidate; living with the consequences can have long-term repercussions that cannot easily be costed. Thus, it becomes essential to ensure that the best candidate is attracted and selected which is equivalent to an investment decision. Rynes et al. (1997) contend that the greater success will be associated with the use of high validity selection devices (Schmidt, Hunter, Mckenzie, & Muldrow, 1979; Schmidt, Hunter, Outerbridge, & Trattner, 1986), the use of more effective recruitment sources (Schwab, 1982; Rynes, 1991), formal evaluation of recruitment process and outcomes (Breaugh, 1992; Cascio, 1989), and taking a longer term strategic perspective on staffing decisions (Breaugh, 1992; Snow & Snell, 1993). Adamsky (2005) summarizes 6 ways the recruiter can help in developing a better organization i.e. hiring good recruiters, branding the organization, rigorously searching talented employees and attracting them to the organization, developing good employee referral programmes, considering talent as opposed to workforce planning, and investing in talented employees. Even if organizations use several recruitment practices at the same time, the effects of such practices have often been studied separately instead of considering all practices together (Rynes, 1991). Thus, not much information or literature is available on how different recruitment practices are related to each other. Hence, second aim is to study various recruitment strategies applied together by the organizations in the context.

A study conducted on information systems employees by Mak & Sockel (2001) states that retention has three indicators viz. employee turnover intention, burnout, and commitment. An employee may develop commitment to the company before joining it (O'Reilly & Caldwell, 1981; Schein, 1968) or at least seen during initial stages of employment (Porter, Crampon, & Smith, 1976). Turnover of an employee does not happen all of a sudden; but this is a process of detachment that can take long time like, several days, weeks, months or even years until the decision to leave actually occurs (Branham, 2005, p.2). Thus, it also becomes essential to understand the employee reactions to recruitment process long after the recruitment process. Perceptions and reactions of applicant recruitment experience have been studied and connected theoretically with results like organizational commitment, job satisfaction, turnover, and organizational climate (Gilliland, 1993). However, dearth of research studies is available in hand that assesses those propositions. Once organizations come to know which results are poor then it would allow organization to suggest improvements in the areas with the greatest chances for overall effectiveness. Thus, this study further intends to understand the applicant reactions to recruitment strategy in terms of the retention indicators.

Recruitment researchers tend to ignore that various companies implement recruitment strategies differently and there are chances that its effectiveness may vary with the organizational context (Rynes & Barber, 1990; Taylor & Collins, 2000). Here, researcher aims to study the effectiveness of recruitment strategy in the context of Indian banking and insurance sector.

It is expected that the continuing changes in the composition of the labour force will have a considerable effect on management in general (Drucker, 1988). By and large economy gives opportunities for variety of employment opportunities. In a rigid economy, employees are unwilling to leave their existing jobs, as generally there are less alternative opportunities available in the market (PSI, 2001). Inflation may also influence recruitment and retention but that relationship is beyond the scope of this research.

The direct implication of this study is that as the competition for recruiting scarce talent has become cut-throat, organizations tend to invest increasingly in lesser expensive retention programs than expensive recruitment efforts to acquire and retain the best and valuable talent.

1.4 Context of the study

Significant growth is witnessed in the Indian service sector, which has been consistently high in India in the last two decades. Banking and insurance sector contributes to about 7% of the country's GDP (Pathak, 2010). Most important of the developments in the financial services, is the surge in the retail banking segment encompassing, multi channel products, multi channel distribution system and multi channel customer and client groups. The government of India liberalized the insurance sector in March 2000, lifting all entry restrictions for private players and allowing foreign players to enter the market with some limits on direct foreign ownership (Pathak, 2010). Insurance industry has witnessed manifold growth with emergence of a number of players from India and abroad offering a wide range of products and several types of insurance policies. At the end of September 2013, there are fifty-two insurance companies operating in India; of which twenty four are in the life insurance business and twenty-seven are in non-life insurance business. In addition, General Insurance Corporation (GIC) is the sole national insurer (IRDA Annual Report, 2012-13). New banking licenses are been cleared by Reserve Bank of India. Significant surge in recruitment activity can be witnessed and one can expect to see rise in poaching within the industry.

Employee attrition rate in Insurance sector is 14%. The rate of attrition is about 35% in the first year of recruitment. This goes down to about 18% by the fourth year (Pathak, 2010). "I would put the churn at the bottom at 100 per cent," says Rajendra Ghag, Senior Executive Vice-President and Chief Human Resource Officer, HDFC Life (Business Line, Jan 2014). In 2012-13 the total number of agents appointed was 5.65 lakhs. The number of agents terminated was as high as 8.01 lakhs (IRDA Annual Report 2012-13).

According to Kelly Services, as stated in Financial Express (Feb, 2014) the attrition rate in banking and financial services industry is expected to be around 18%. It was same i.e. 18 per cent in the year 2010-11. The number of bank employees in Indian private sector banks rose to 2,18,679 in 2010-11 from 1,82,520 according to the 'Statistical Tables Relating to Banks of India released by the Reserve Bank of India in 2012. But the same was reduced in foreign banks from 28,012 in 2009-10 to 27,968 in 2010-11. Banking and insurance is mainly people-oriented business and human resources play very important role in differentiating the business.

Most of the insurance companies have tied up with foreign insurance companies. Insurance business is growing rapidly in India. This has created a pressure on recruitment managers of these insurance companies to recruit rigorously in the business. Therefore, the basic aim of the recruitment manager is to fill up the positions. This has led to insufficient attention to strategy designing for hiring employees who could stay with the organization for longer time. Initially, these private sector insurance companies hired employees by poaching in public sector insurance companies. But the growth was very high and number of insurance companies started emerging in the Indian market. Again these organizations started poaching in other private sector insurance companies to fill in their positions. Few insurance companies hired people for sales positions from BPOs. This has created a 'war of talent' in Indian insurance sector. Therefore, it becomes necessary to study recruitment strategy of such insurance companies to understand retention in the same. It has also been revealed through different studies that the need of growing employee requirement is not fulfilled merely by adopting some retention strategies rather it is equally important to identify the right candidates at the time of recruitment, so that they identify with the organization and stay on proving to be assets for the company. This study attempts to identify the way recruitment strategy is implemented in banking and insurance organizations and then find if the same is related to kind of employees retained in the organization.

As the rate of attrition is high in private sector banks and insurance companies, this study is conducted considering the same. Indian public sector organizations have more structured and transparent recruitment policy, which makes recruitment systematic, and attrition rate in these organizations is low so these organizations are excluded from the study.

1.5 Research Problem

Research problem is stated as 'Study of recruitment strategy applied by Indian private sector banks and insurance companies with reference to the type of employees retained in the same organizations'.

1.6 Objectives of Study

The research objectives are stated as follows:

1. To study recruitment strategies adopted by the organizations in Indian Banking and Insurance Sector.
2. To study employee retention in the Indian Banking and Insurance Sector.
3. To study the relationship between each element of recruitment strategy and each of the categories of employee retention in the Indian Banking and Insurance Sector.

1.7 Scope and Delimitations of the Study

The study is cross-sectional in design, thus restricting causal inferences or attributions. Attention should also be drawn to the fact that the data is collected from employees of their up to 5 years of tenure in the current organization. This might limit the capacity of respondents, who have spent more than 1 year, to recollect their recruitment experience and answer accurately.

Further, Rynes et al. (1997) have viewed that when data are gathered from applicants alone, there is no opportunity to link applicant perceptions of recruiters to organizational recruitment practices, or to nonsuperficial recruiter characteristics such as attitudes and beliefs (Connerley, 1997). Instead, usual 'applicant impression' studies have merely linked respondents' overall impressions of recruiter effectiveness with their impressions of effectiveness on specific dimensions.

The scope of the study is recruitment strategy and employee retention in Indian banking and insurance sector. Thus, factors other than recruitment strategy influencing employee retention are not considered for the study.

Study investigated private, co-operative and foreign banks and private and foreign insurance companies operating in India, thus prohibiting meaningful assessment of how recruitment strategy and employee retention, and their linkages vary among other sectors.

1.8 Significance of study

The study will be useful to academics as well as industry in several manners. The study is important from the point of view of understanding theoretical foundations of recruitment strategy and employee retention. This study helps to understand recruitment strategy in a holistic manner with empirical support.

Understanding the nature of employee retention with reference to recruitment experience is possible at the end of this research study. The nature of recruitment and retention in Indian banking and insurance sector is studied with the help of this study.

In order to conduct this research the review of earlier work is essential. Hence review of literature is done and presented in the next chapter

CHAPTER II

REVIEW OF LITERATURE

2.1 Chapter Overview

This chapter covers related literature on theoretical foundations of strategy, recruitment strategy, and employee retention. Considering related literature, gaps in the research are identified. The same is followed by list of variables under study and its operational definitions. It also includes hypotheses of the study. At the end, concept map is presented.

Before reviewing related literature it becomes essential to understand the theoretical foundations of strategy, recruitment strategy and employee retention.

2.2 Theoretical Foundations

2.2.1 Strategy

The term *strategy* within human resources management, as well as in general, is often used, seldom clarified, and frequently assumed to be one-dimensional. According to Mintzberg (1978), the term *strategy* is typically used to define the deliberate and conscious act of planning for the future. However, this is limiting and arguably inappropriate. Mintzberg (1978) elaborates: "…

by restricting strategy to explicit, a priori guidelines, it forces the researcher to study strategy formation as a perceptual phenomenon, all too often reducing his [her] conclusions to abstract normative generalizations."

A brilliant strategy may put you on the competitive map. But only solid execution keeps you there (Neilson et al. 2011). Strategy in general and realized strategy in particular, is defined by Buck and Watson (2002) as a pattern in a stream of decisions. The realized strategies are not necessarily the same as the intended strategies, but rather represent the strategies that have evolved based upon implemented policies and practices. In other words, when a sequence of decisions in some area exhibits a consistency over time, a strategy will be considered to have formed. Porter (2011) contends that operational effectiveness is different from strategic positioning. Operational effectiveness is performing activities faster, or with fewer inputs and lesser defects than the other competitors. Strategic positioning is performing different activities from rivals, or performing similar activities in different ways. It attempts to achieve sustainable competitive advantage by preserving what is distinctive about a company. He further explains three principles underlying Strategic Positioning. They are: a) Strategy is a creation of a unique and valuable position, involving a different set of activities. b) Strategy requires one to make trade-offs in competing – to choose what not to do. c) Strategy involves creating 'fit' among a company's activities (Porter, 2011).

The strategy perspective can be further explained in the context of Human Resource Management (HRM) activities.

2.2.2 Strategic HRM (SHRM) and HRM Strategy

Snell, Youndt, and Wright (1996) viewed Strategic HRM as "organizational systems designed to achieve sustainable competitive advantage through people". Ulrich (1997) describes

Strategic HRM as "the process of linking HR practices to business strategy". HRM strategy involves identifying those HR capabilities needed to implement business strategy and adapting those HR practices and policies for gaining those capabilities. The process of Strategic HRM is a goal-directed (Wright & McMahan, 1992). Therefore, researchers should evaluate the extent to which those goals and objectives are achieved through the process implemented for the same. (Becker & Gerhart, 1996; Kaplan & Norton, 2001; Steers, 1975).

According to Bamberger & Meshoulam (2000) there is likely to be a difference between a firm's "espoused" HR strategy and its "emergent" strategy. Espoused HR strategy is the pattern of HR-related decisions made but not necessarily implemented. It is often explicated as part of "corporate philosophy" or included as a central component of a managerial mission statement. In contrast, the emergent HR strategy is the pattern of HR-related decisions that, although perhaps never made explicit, have in fact been applied: that is the gestalt of negotiated people-related policies and practices in use.

Buck and Watson (2002) define 'realized HRM' strategies as the manner in which the institution handles generic aspects of the relationship between the employer and the employee. These generic aspects can include the degree of decentralization, the compensation method, the employees' participation programs levels, the degree of training and development activities, the skill-sets of employees and the system of social interactions within the organization. These generic aspects can be examined individually or holistically as a system. The realized strategies are not necessarily the same as the 'intended strategies', but rather represent the strategies that have evolved based upon implemented policies and practices.

Human Resource Management (HRM) strategies define how the HRM function and and in what manner organization's human resources should help in achieving organizational goals and objectives. When HRM provides opinion and comments about the ability of SHRM in contributing attainment of organizational goals and objectives, the degree of vertical structural alignment is expected to be greatest (Lengnick-Hall and Lengnick-Hall, 1988).

Model by CIPD (2001) given in figure 2.1 depicts that HR practices leads to HR outcomes. HR practices can be various recruitment practices adopted by the organizations and outcomes can be the level of commitment or turnover intent of the employees.

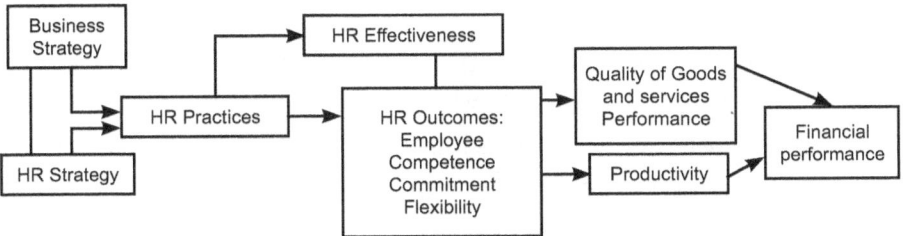

Figure 2.1: Model of the link between HRM and Performance – Source CIPD, 2001

It becomes essential to understand founding theories of Human Resource Management. The same can be briefly explained below:

Socialization Theory

Socialization theory investigates an organization's culture, values, beliefs, and practices (Wanous *et al,* 1984). Organizational socialization helps prospective candidates with certain valuable data about work profile and the organizational culture in order to facilitate an effective person/job match (Adkins, 1995). Therefore, certain recruitment practices like employee referrals give prospective candidates up-front organizational and job related information. It is seen in the research studies that both perceived and actual organizational fit affect an employees' approach toward leaving an organization (Ravlin and Ritchie, 2006), and that socialization strategies help to hold the employee into the organization and reduce turnover (Allen, 2006).

Resource-based view

Resource-based view (RBV) theory has strong implications for SHRM (Wright, Dunford, & Snell, 2001). It gives theoretical viewpoint from which organizational science research can consider internal organizational resources as a basis for sustainable competitive advantage (Barney, Wright, & Ketchen, 2001). Based on Barney's work Wright and McMahan (1992) contended that if four basic requirements are fulfilled, human resources can be considered as a source of sustained competitive advantage. First, they must add value to the firm's production processes. Second, the skill set that the firm wants to seek must be rare. Third, firm's combined human capital investments in the form of employees cannot be easily imitated. Finally, to provide a source of sustainable competitive advantage, firm's resources must not cause the experience replacement by technological developments or other substitutes.

The multiple stakeholder perspective

The multiple stakeholder perspective explains conceptual framework that can improve our ability to correctly define and measure organizational effectiveness (Freeman, 1984, 1985; Schuler & Jackson, 1999; Freeman & McVea, 2001). The systems theory involves underlying assumption behind the integration of a multiple stakeholder perspective in SHRM research. The systems theory (Ackoff, 1970, 1974; Buckley, 1967) lay emphasis on the view that organizations are open systems rather than independent ones which requires the support of both external and internal stakeholders in order to effectively deal with relevant organizational issues and problems (Freeman & McVea, 2001).

The concepts of vertical and horizontal linkage

The HRM practices deployed by the organization must be linked with various organizational resources to create value, generate sustainable competitive advantage, and improve organizational effectiveness (Delery, 1998; Delery & Doty, 1996; Huselid et al., 1997).

Systematic agreement theory (SAT)

According to Semler (1997) systematic agreement theory (SAT) presents a structure in which organizational alignment – i.e., the degree to which an organization's design, strategies, and culture are assisting to attain the same desired goals. Such alignment is proposed to enhance organizational effectiveness in the form of accomplishment of organizational goals and objectives and create competitive advantage (Semler, 1997). Given below are few types of alignments:

A. Structural alignment

Structural alignment refers to the congruency between the objectives of different organizational activities or processes and the way SHRM is intended to bring forth the behaviours necessary to meet those objectives (Semler, 1997). Consequently, vertical structural alignment refers to the degree to which the goals, objectives, and strategies for important organizational processes are harmonizing throughout the organization for these processes to add value toward the achievement of the goals and objectives of the organization as a whole (Kaplan & Norton, 2001; Semler, 1997). Horizontal structural alignment refers to the extent to which an organization elicits behaviours or outcomes from its personnel resources that are in congruence with those behaviours or outcomes necessary for the attainment of organizational goals and objectives (Schuler & Jackson,

1987; Wright, 1998). Such horizontal structural alignment is realized through two important fundamentals: The first important fundamental of horizontal alignment entails staffing (e.g. hiring and selection), developing (e.g., training programs), retaining (e.g., performance appraisal and management) and empowering (e.g., self-directed teams) a labor force (Way, 2002; Wright & Snell, 1998). The second important fundamental of horizontal alignment includes motivating these human resources by way of performance-based compensation (Way, 2002; Wright & Snell, 1998).

B. Cultural alignment

Cultural alignment refers to the way an organization's leadership over and above SHRM stimulates an organizational culture to support strategies of the organization and helps achieve goals and objectives of the organization (Semler, 1997).

C. Performance alignment

Performance alignment refers to the degree to which the organization's real results are equivalent to those results important for the organization to achieve its goals and objectives (Semler, 1997).

D. Environmental alignment

The last characteristic of SAT is environmental alignment, which replicates the strategic fit between the needs of the external environment and the chosen vision, goals, and tactics of the organization (Semler, 1997).

Strategic Reference Points Theory (SRPT)

SRPT has a strong conceptual framework that integrates three significant dimensions related to alignment: (i) internal circumstances of the organization; (ii) external circumstances of the organization; and (iii) time (Fiegenbaum, Hart, & Schendel, 1996).

The competitive business environment of 21st century reflects the factors such as aging and changing workforce in a high technology workplace that demands and rewards the ever-increasing skill and increased global competition in almost every sector of the economy. Human resources represent a quantitative and qualitative measurement of the workforce required in an organisation. The effective management of these human factors is required for the success of an organisation. An example of the impact of the HR function on the organisation can be seen from a Hewitt research paper that states that a 10% increase in attracting and retaining pivotal employees adds approximately $70 to $160 million to a large-sized company's bottom line. An area of concern for HR is that our tools and techniques are not consistently applied. Finance has balance sheets and P&L accounts, marketers have Boston boxes and STP, strategists have 'five-forces analysis' GE strategic positioning matrices and value chains, and so on. HR tools needed for strategic input vary from organization to organization – there is not even an agreed way of reporting headcount (staff working flexible hours, for example). This means that a common understanding of how HR should intervene does not exist, making for fragmented and inconsistent approach. There is a need to rectify this by having a generic form of strategic intervention – at the very least, some tools techniques that can be agree as best practice. Though less there are few studies on recruitment strategy that can be described in the following sections.

2.2.3 Recruitment Strategy

Adding a new person to workforce of an organization is one of the crucial decisions. The process of recruitment emerges as one of the most critical and strategic process in any organization. Recruitment strategy of a firm is defined as an organizational decision making processes in which several departments (personnel management, first-line managers) are involved (Windolf, 1986). Christopher Lewis (1985) has distinguished between recruitment and selection along with definitions of both the terms. According to him, "Recruitment is the activity that generates a pool of applicants, who have the desire to be employed by the organization, from which those suitable can be selected". He defines Selection as, "The activity in which an organization uses one or more methods to assess individuals with a view to making a decision concerning their suitability to join that organization, to perform tasks which may or may not be specified". It can be seen from the definitions that the first stage of the process is labelled recruitment, and second selection. But there are clearly selection activities in the early stages – for example, specifying necessary academic qualifications in job advertisements- and recruitment activities in the later stages – for example, using a selection interview to persuade good applicant that he ought to join the organization. Boudreau and Rynes (1985) explain distinction between recruitment and selection. They define *Recruitment* "as activities or practices that alter the characteristics of applicants to whom selection procedures are ultimately applied". "Selection in turn, involves evaluating predictor information for purposes of making a final hiring decision".

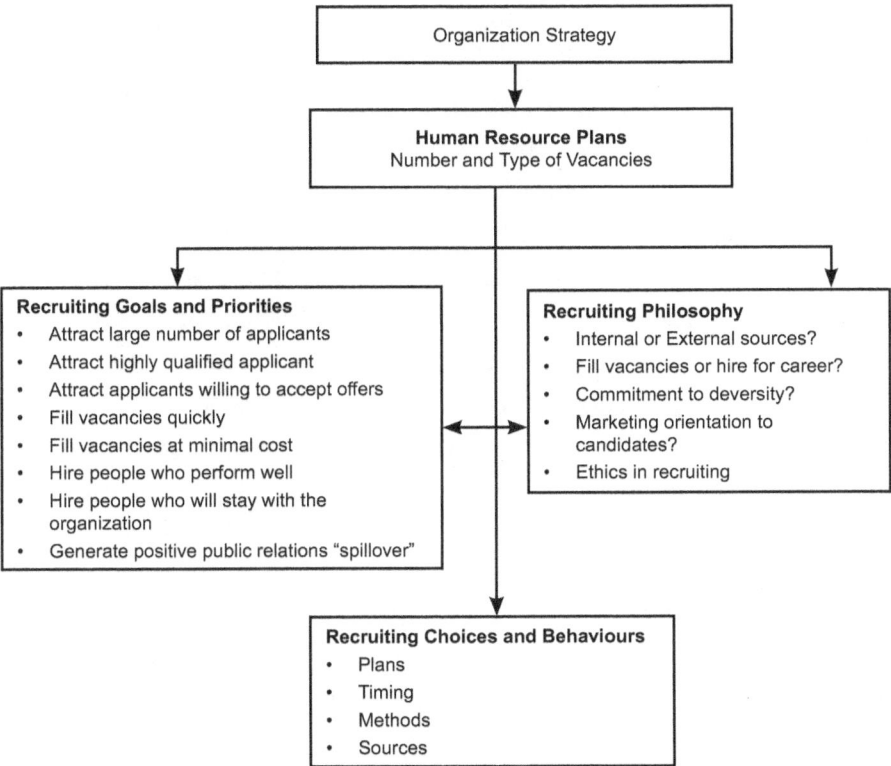

Figure 2.2: Organizational strategy

Paul Windolf (1986) contends that the selection of a specific recruitment strategy is dependent on both environmental constraints like labour market power and the internal resources like organizational intelligence of the organization which further leads to the kind of workers recruited in the organization. The supremacy of the organization in the personnel market decides the scale of choice which the organization can put into effect in deciding a specific recruitment strategy. Organizational intelligence describes the competence of the firm to use professional knowledge, to gather and process information, and to design multifaceted labour market strategies. Figure 2.2 shows various strategic decisions made while performing recruitment function in the organization (**Fisher et al, 2005**)

Windolf (1986) further highlights on four recruitment strategies that might be useful for the organizations. Firstly, in the innovative strategy the firm tries to attract the possible potential 'innovators'. Secondly, the status-quo strategy, which is exclusively oriented towards its traditional market segments. It tends to employ people with similar degree of skill and professional experience, from the same social status and with a similar social background, age, and sex as those already employed in the company. Thirdly, the Autonomous strategy follows recruitment process with accurate definition of the ideal candidate in terms of age, sex, and professional experience. Skills, age, and job experience are usually specified within a narrow range. The firm refrains to adapt its requirements to prevailing market conditions. Neither unemployment nor full employment is likely to change the demand structure of such firms. They 'skim off' the market because they are at the forefront leading the queue of employers in the labour market. Finally, the flexible/muddling-through strategy of firm does not typically enter the market with a specific outline of the ideal candidate rather it screens the market to 'see what is available'. Once market information is obtained, the firm decides how to reframe its own division of labour and whether training has to be given.

Rynes (1991) defined recruiting as encompassing "all organizational activities and decisions that affect either the number or types of individuals who are willing to apply for, or to accept, a vacancy". Myres (1992) defines recruitment as the human resource management activity of developing external and internal sources of qualified applicants. Actually it is a combination of activities that can be manipulated independently. Barber (1998) pointed out that the first phase of recruitment as the period when a firm uses an array of different practices to attract individuals to apply to the organization. In addition, success of an organization in its early stage of recruitment restrains the supreme value of the recruitment process as a whole because the effectiveness of succeeding recruitment operations can only make or mar the size and quality of the initial applicant pool (Carison, Connerley, & Mecham, 2002). Recruitment is an organization's way of actively reaching out and inviting applicants **(Berry 2003)**. It is the process by which organizations locate and attract individuals to fill job vacancies.

Past Recruitment Research

Varieties of researchers have worked on recruitment practices, recruitment effectiveness, and applicant reactions to recruitment process. Their research work can be explained chronologically. Schneider (1987) has hypothesized that people are a function of the attraction-selection-attrition (ASA) cycle, which is a model that proposes individuals with similar personality and values are *attracted* to certain organizations and *selected* by these organizations. People who do not agree with the patterns and values expressed by the organization will eventually leave (*attrition*). This ASA framework suggests that the recruitment activities that an organization utilizes greatly impact the created applicant pool. The vital aim of the recruitment process is for the participating parties viz. interviewers and candidates to negotiate a "psychological contract" (Herriot, 1989). In addition to justice considerations, the "psychological contract" model includes perceptions of one's affective and cognitive conditions during the process and their general perceptions about testing and hiring as probable determining factors of personal and organizational results. This can be done by stating their respective expectations, assuming them, or inferring them.

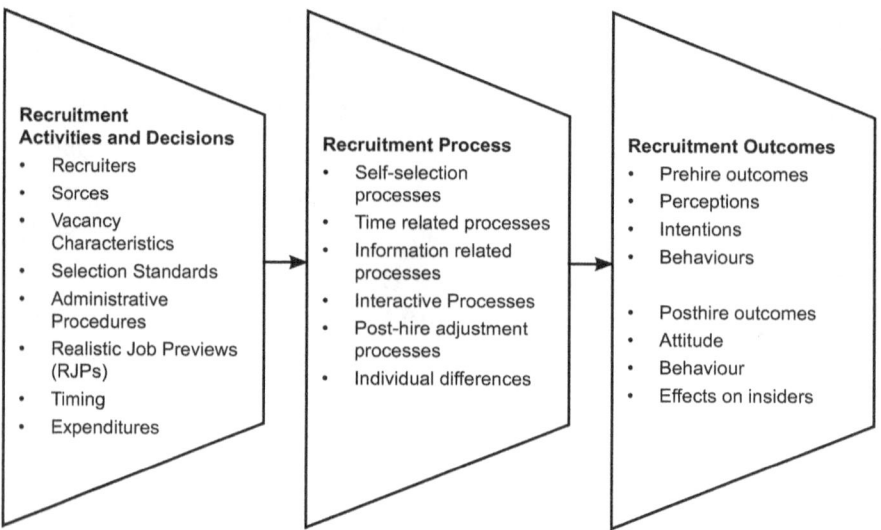

Figure 2.3 Model for future recruitment research –Sara Rynes, 1989

At the same time Sara Rynes (1989) anticipated that recruitment research might become a more fundamental factor in determining recruitment practices if it were to ask more critical questions, such that it should be designed to answer the critical questions, frame new set of questions and show results, no matter how specific, in relation to the broader recruitment context and environment they are. After reviewing past research she helps researchers with model for future recruitment research. The model given in figure 2.3 above which states that future research should consider the way recruitment activities lead to recruitment processes, and how the same affects recruitment outcomes.

Rynes and Barber (1990) and Rynes (1991) have criticized recruitment research on methodological ground, i.e., of being very naive and not capturing the real world complexities thus being unrealistic. Prominently, much of the empirical research have relied on candidates' perceptions of job attributes and recruiting practices composed simultaneously. Powell (1991) proposes the importance of additional longitudinal research before any definitive conclusions about the long-term effects of recruiting practices can be reached.

As an extension to the HRM strategy theories, Organizational justice theory explains how applicants' perceptions towards justice develop and later on change various outcomes in selection situations (Gilliland, 1993). This theory involves the perceived fairness of (Greenberg, 1993):

 i. Outcome allocations (distributive justice),
 ii. Rules and procedures used to make those decisions (procedural justice),
 iii. Sensitivity and respect shown to individuals (interpersonal justice), and
 iv. Explanations and accounts given to individuals (informational justice).

These perceptions affect future attitudes, intentions, self-perceptions, and behaviours of employees. Applicant reactions are often operationalized using procedural justice dimensions. According to the "procedural justice theory" (Gilliland, 1993), the applicants identify and assess the selection process in considering its fairness, viz, their satisfaction or violation of a certain set of specific procedural norms which are related to face validity, as well as communication and interpersonal behaviour. Procedural justice perceptions during recruitment process seems to relate to important outcomes for the organization, such as organizational commitment (Robertson et al. 1991), organizational attractiveness and recommendation that the candidates make to others related to the company (Smither et al. 1993). Procedural justice perceptions forecast employee behavioural patterns such as job satisfaction, commitment, turnover, and their performances (Konovsky & Cropanzano, 1991). Even though research convinces that the result of the selection process is a more important factor determining the organizational outcomes than the perceptions of the transparency of the process, perceptions in relation to procedural justice still envisage organizational outcomes beyond selection process results (Bauer et al., 1998). Hence, the finest research design should also include post-result outcomes of applicant reactions.

Newton (1998) suggests that the recruitment process is not just a function of the organization, but rather an interactive process where both the organization representative and the applicant make decisions. While explaining the recruitment process, Barber (1998) outlined three phases i.e., generating applicants, maintaining applicant status, and influencing their job choice decisions. That is, (a) specific recruitment practices may influence the number and type of individuals who apply for an organization, (b) few activities may force applicants to leave during the recruitment process, and (c) few more recruitment actions may decide whether a job offer is accepted or not.

Next attempt to theoretically connect recruitment practices with candidates' responses hails from the person-perception theory. It enhances upon primary theoretical structure to include additional antecedent and moderator variables (Ryan & Polyhart, 2000). Breaugh and Starke (2000) explain a model of organizational recruitment process in their seminal paper. This paper talks about recruitment objectives, strategy development, recruitment activities, and intervening process variables resulting in recruitment outcomes.

Hausknecht et al. (2004) in their study points out that applicant with positive perceptions about recruitment process are more likely to see organization positively and show eagerness to accept job offers. They developed an updated model of applicant reactions to selection process. This model proposes that vital results can be best predicted by perception of applicants towards selection process. Those relevant results include recruitment practices performance, self-perceptions, and different of attitudes and behaviours like commitment and turnover intent. Perception of applicant takes into consideration various dimensions of organizational justice, thoughts and feelings and attitudes about recruitment testing and hiring process. This model can be depicted in figure 2.4. In this theoretical model, Hausknecht, et al. (2004) measured both organizational justice perspective and attribution theory. The authors contended that it was not precise whether applicants see the hiring practices through a justice or attributional lens. They summarized that fairness perception, attributions towards the organization, or both may influence applicants' reactions if there is a long delay in such situations. eg. Few applicants who experience unwarranted delays may not like the process and form negative perceptions towards the organizations without viewing the process as unfair.

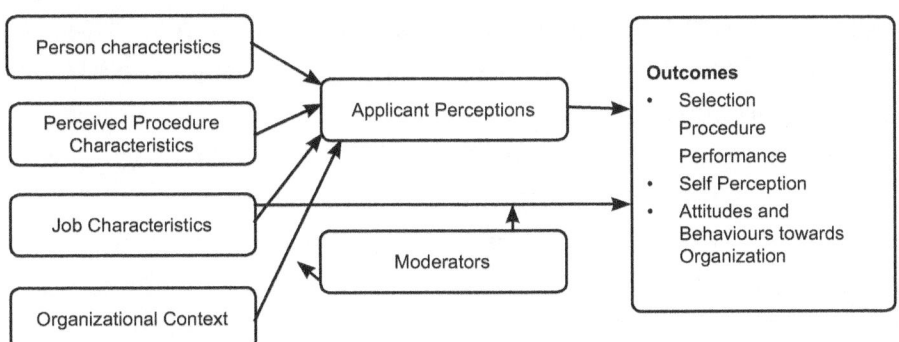

Figure 2.4 Updated Theoretical Model of Applicant Reactions to Selection - Hausknecht et al., 2004

2.3 Cost Considerations

After considering theoretical foundations it also becomes necessary to understand the cost involvement in recruiting activity. Literature mainly depicts two types of costs i.e. Cost of Turnover and Cost of Recruitment. Literature on both can be explained as follows:

2.3.1 Cost of Turnover

Measuring the cost of employee turnover can be a real challenge. It is not only a significant tangible dollar cost but also an intangible or "hidden" cost associated with loss of skills, inefficiency and replacement costs (Lashley and Chaplain, 1999). Unnecessary employee turnover costs organizations needless expenses (Soloman, as cited in Rust, Stewart, Miller, & Pielack, 1996). Soloman found that "separation, replacement, and training costs are estimated 1.5 to 2.5 times of annual salary for each person who quits".

Voluntary and involuntary turnover of employees involve costs of separation, recruitment and training and job search for both the firm and the employee (Cascio, 1991). Hinkin and Tracey (2000) designed a computer program to assess the cost of employee turnover. This program includes of variables that calculate the total direct cost viz. advertising, signing bonuses and formal training and indirect costs viz. lowered productivity of newly joined employees and interruption to the working of existing employees of turnover. The direct costs of employee turnover are normally categorised into three main sections: cost of separation (exit interviews, administration, functions related to terminations, separation pay, and unemployment tax), cost of replacement (communicating job vacancies, pre-employment administrative functions, interviews, and exams), and costs of training (formal classroom training and on-the-job instruction) (Slaughter and Ang, 1996). The component of indirect costs included in employee turnover are more difficult to study and include the loss of efficiency of employees before actual turnover takes place, the effect on their co-workers' productivity, and the loss of productivity before a new employee gets excellence in the job undertaken (Blankertz and Robinson, 1997).

In addition to actual loss of rupee, replacement and training expenses have a staggering impact on organizational costs, productivity, and performance. An increasing number of organizations are now realizing that the employee retention is an important strategic issue (Glen, 2006).

Many other researchers have contended that the costs of turnover includes the expenses like recruitment and training of employees (Alexander, Bloom, & Nichols, 1994), loss of social capital at firm-level (Dess & Shaw, 2001), reduction in transitory productivity (Osterman, 1987), and loss of important tacit knowledge (Droege & Hoobler, 2003).

2.3.2 Cost of Recruitment

Involvement in recruiting (including advertising), training, induction, growth and skill development, and quality represent a direct cost of recruiting to the organisation (Hinkin and Tracey, 2006). Actually hiring employees is very expensive as it involves interviews, drug tests, background checks, training, overtime for current employees, lost productivity, temporary workers, etc.

To assess return on the investment of recruitment processes and services, employer should take into consideration various 'hidden costs' that an ideal recruitment device can avoid. Employee effectiveness must be assessed as per true cost-per-hire analysis. Punia and Sharma (2008) suggest that further concentration must be given to both the residual effects of recruitment campaigns and the cost of marketing for building company branding. Reduction in cost of the composite recruitment process must be viewed as worthwhile by management and this objective may be attained by precise targeting of candidates, rather than the adoption of a blanket approach towards securing the employee (Sommerville, 1996).

With these theoretical perspectives in mind, let us now turn attention to variables of study.

2.4 Recruitment Strategy Variables

Number of researchers have studied variety of recruitment variables and their effectiveness in different research contexts. Recruitment strategy involves variety of decisions taken by the organization in order to attain their strategic objectives. The strategic decisions taken by organization are implemented in the form of operational processes. Those processes that are experienced by the applicants during recruitment activities are considered for study in this research.

2.4.1 Information Shared

One of the strategic decisions organization can take during recruitment process is what and how much information to be given out to attract potential applicants. A recruitment message that describes the similarities between likely applicants and the organization's current workforce is based on a person–group fit perspective. It recommends that ideal applicants will be more attracted to organizations with employees similar to themselves (Kristof-Brown et al., 2005). The focal point of realistic recruitment theory is retention of employee rather than attracting applicants (Rynes, 1989). Realistic recruitment theory hypothesizes that traditional strategy for applicant attraction may have damaging effects on succeeding efforts of employee retention. Literature on information shared is termed differently by different authors. Few call it as recruitment message, few as recruitment communication, and few as information shared during recruitment.

The purpose of the recruitment message is to provide the potential applicant with specific job attributes to encourage them to apply for the position. Recruitment message is the recruitment activity that attempts to encourage the applicant to take the first step to learn more about the employment opportunity. Once applicant is into the recruitment process he seeks more information about the job and organization. The recruitment message generally contains such information as job description, required experience, salary, benefits, job specifications, and the work schedule. More detailed recruitment message may contain information about the company, work environment, local community, and possibilities for advancement. Such recruitment information is made available through variety of media like newspapers, trade magazines, on the Internet and communicated by recruiters, interviewers and / or current employees.

It is not just important to understand what and how much information is shared by the organization to applicants but it is also essential to understand various other attributes of information shared. Important attributes studied by various researchers are: realistic (e.g. Realistic Job Preview - RJP), specificity, trustworthiness, accuracy of information, breadth and timeliness of information shared. Out of these attributes researchers have given greater attention to RJP or sharing realistic information during recruitment process. Meyer *et al.,* (2003) have emphasized that 'realistic job previews' provide potential new hires with more than just cursory glance at company's operations, providing the candidate with enough information to make a decision about whether it is the right workplace for him/her. Such information shared at the time of recruitment is believed to function as a realistic job preview and to reduce turnover.

_The literature on recruitment message covers basically two types of recruitment messages: realistic messages and inflated, 'sales-oriented,' or 'flypaper'-type messages. Employers frequently take advantage of job seekers' uncertainty by overselling vacancies (Schneider, 1976), perhaps at the expense of subsequent employee satisfaction and turnover. Wanous (1973) concludes that those applicants who received realistic job preview had higher survival rates and better job performance. He further contends (1980) that RJP is an approach which assumes that giving candidates / newcomers accurate and complete information will results in better matching, increased satisfaction and commitment, and lower turnover. He also suggests that such realistic information can be conveyed through booklets, films, video-tapes, realistic work-samples, interviewers, supervisors, other recent hires, and a combination of these approaches. Reilly et al. (1981) contend that on average, the turnover rate for realistically recruited employees was 5.7 percentage points lower than that for employees recruited through more conventional messages. Malatesta (1981) summarized results of eleven studies and brought into focus a significant negative relationship between realistic job information and turnover. As per Taylor & Schmidt (1983) RJP helps reduce turnover (1) by permitting applicants to "self select" themselves out of consideration for a position they feel would not satisfy their needs; (2) by lowering their expectations about job conditions, thus increasing satisfaction once on the job; (3) by increasing their levels of organizational commitment because the job offer was accepted voluntarily without strong inducements; and (4) by increasing their ability to cope with unpleasant job demands. Reilly et al. (1985) reviewed fifteen realistic preview studies designed to evaluate effects on turnover. The study showed an average correlation between realism and retention. On average, those candidates who received realistic previews had turnover rates of 30%, as compared with 40% for control groups. Job characteristics described in the recruitment message have a significant impact on the reaction of job applicants to recruitment stimuli on two ways: 1) failing to provide job-related information resulted in less favourable applicant perception of the recruitment message, and b) the nature of job attributes influenced applicant reaction to the recruitment message (Rynes, 1991). RJPs are relatively inexpensive to develop and implement, and the payoff of even small effects can be great in terms of lower selection and turnover costs (Breaugh, 1992; Dean & Wanous, 1984). The study by Saks (1994) suggested that realistic job previews and job expectations were important for understanding the relationship between job survival and recruitment sources. Similarly, the results of study by Phillips (1998) suggest that RJPs are related to lower levels of voluntary turnover.

Apart from being realistic it is important to provide sufficient and truthful depiction of the company's culture so that it helps candidates to decide if their values match those of the organization (Cameron and Quinn, 1999; Trice and Beyer, 1993; Schein, 1977). Recruitment messages that provide unambiguous or detailed information turn out to be more favourable than do non-specific or general messages. E.g., Rynes and Miller (1983) showed that greater than before amounts of information regarding specific job characteristics (e.g., salary, career paths and benefits) positively influenced perceptions of applicants' about organizational attractiveness. Breaugh and Billings (1988) contended that, many times when an employer tried to give realistic job information, frequently the information presented was so general ("salaries are competitive") that it did not help candidates for informed recruitment decision-making. Similarly, it was hypothesized and confirmed by Barber and Roehling (1993) that candidates give more attention to specific than to general information.

Communication during recruitment is expected to be understandable and viewed as trustworthy by the candidates whom the organization is interested in recruiting (Breaugh & Biliings, 1988). In case of credibility of information shared, previous research has revealed that receiving information that is different than that expected from the message source results in credibility (Stiff, 1994). Stiff (1994) has constantly shown that proficiency of communicator and his trustworthiness direct a message's being believed. The accuracy of information obtained through the recruitment source significantly impacted job survival. Therefore, the authors argued that importance is placed on the organization to present information that is accurate with the hopes of decreasing employee turnover. The message being sent out by the organization needs to be appealing, but also accurate (Dale, 1999). Thus, the provision of reliable information reduces turnover and increases the value of the match.

Rynes et al. (1991) further focused upon the timing of recruitment communications in terms of signaling. These authors hypothesized that delays in responding to application inquiries or it making job offers may be viewed as a signal that the organization does not have a strong interest in the candidate. The study by Phillips (1998) also revealed moderating effects of the timing of an RJP, the medium used for the RJP, and whether the research in which a given RJP was assessed was conducted in the laboratory or the field was found for the relationships between RJPs and attrition from recruitment, job satisfaction, organizational commitment, and voluntary turnover. Thus, by avoiding delays between recruitment stages, employers can minimize the chances of discouraging applicants, and have long term effect on the applicants like increased loyalty. Chapman et al.'s (2005) meta-analysis has found that timely response by the organization was included as subcategory of justice perceptions, and longer delays in communication during recruitment were found to have a negative effect on organizational attraction. Rynes, Bretz, & Gerhart (1991) and Chapman & Webster (2006) found that post interview delays in communicating with candidates led to negative perceptions of the organization.

Fisher et al. (1979) found that employees and friends as sources of employment information had comparable effects:

both were more credible and influential than recruiters. People who are unhappy in their jobs may blame that unhappiness on having had inadequate information before they accepted rather than on poor personal decision-making. Organizations may for many reasons put pressures on hiring or particular reward systems, for instance-present unrealistically positive pictures of jobs, individuals may need to draw on information from many sources both inside and outside organizations to develop accurate pictures of jobs and their settings (Louis, 1980). The commitment hypothesis suggests that people develop stronger commitment to organizations that give them the information they need to make fully informed job choices (Rynes, 1989). Rynes with other colleagues found that prior knowledge of a company moderated the effectiveness of recruitment practices (Rynes, Bretz, and Gerhart, 1991). According to Phillips, job previewing is a cost saving activity as well. Bamberger & Meshoulam (2000) contend that a realistic recruitment philosophy is likely to yield positive strategic effects on to the extent that it increases the rate of applicant retention without reducing the quality of those candidates available for hire.

Even though researchers have given more attention to whether a recruitment message includes realistic as opposed to only positive information (Phillips, 1998), three other important attributes of message (i.e., the breadth of topics addressed, the specificity of the information provided, the timing of communications) worth attention by researchers (Breaugh and Starke, 2000).

2.4.2 Recruitment Process Experience

Herriot (1988) contends that during recruitment both parties i.e. recruiter and candidate make the false assumption of "low distinctiveness", i.e., they both consider that behavior of people in work life is similar to the way they present during the interview.

Attribution theory can be applied to recruiter behaviour during such recruitment process. In such a context, the applicant may generalize the recruiter's behaviour to the whole organization and, hence, the recruiter plays very important role in signifying what other members of the organization are like, as well as, what the organization is like (Rynes, 1989). Breaugh (1992) believe that recruitment research would benefit from studies that collect more process-rich information about the dynamics of recruitment decision-making. According to Applicant Attribution – Reaction Theory (AART) (Polyhart & Harold, 2004), candidates who apply to the organization generally form false and automatic perceptions during various stages of selection process. AART put forwards that negative attributions gives rise to prejudice in perceptions and also behavioural outcomes, such as withdrawal from the recruitment and selection process and denial of job proposal.

A majority of the research related to recruiters has attempted to find out what are various recruiter characteristics that give an explanation for applicants overall impressions of recruiter. Various researchers have given different clarifications on why applicants get affected by recruiters' behavior. They have contended that candidates are highly influenced by recruiters in the organization (Rynes, Heneman, & Schwab, 1980; Schmitt & Coyle, 1976). Rynes (1991) also contended that recruiters might influence candidates because applicants view them as indicator of unknown organizational characteristics. In addition to that, it has been seen that such impressions many times influence applicants approach towards successive stages of the recruitment process, and also their decision of job choices (Harris & Fink, 1987; Rynes, Bretz, & Gerhart, 1991). Sometimes no direct consequence of recruiter attributes are seen on perceived employment opportunities but the same may have an indirect influence through their impact on job attributes (Harris & fink, 1987). Therefore, it is required to entirely scrutinize the consequence of recruiters' behaviour on candidates. Considering past studies Harris & Fink (1987) tested four categories of recruiter characteristics. They are personableness, competence, informativeness, and aggressiveness. Personableness and informativeness came out as the most significant characteristics of recruiters. Their study showed that recruiter characteristics were considerably linked to the regard for the organization.

The first of these characteristics has to do with recruiter informativeness. How informed and informative the recruiter is influences applicant reactions (Harris & Fink, 1987; Turban & Dougherty, 1992). Powell (1991) has hypothesized that a few recruiters in the organization present more information and more specific information to candidates than the other recruiters. Knowing that the kind of information shared is of personal significance to the job applicant and is assumed, conversing with more informative recruiters should have several positive outcomes e.g., improved ability of candidates to withdraw from the job assignment that eventually would not be rewarding. Considering recruiter informativeness, it has been recommended (Breaugh, 1992) that as candidate's forthcoming superior or co-workers should be particularly informative compared to the other recruiters (e.g. anyone from the Human Resources department) who may not hold as much information expected by the candidates. With regard to recruiter informativeness, it is the extent to which the information communicated by an organizational recruiter contains allocation of realistic as against to the only affirmative information (Connerley & Rynes, 1997).

Connerley & Rynes (1997) have recommended that personableness of recruiter may be significant because it is an indicator of how the candidate may be treated if selected by the organization or how likely the candidate is to get an offer of job.

A study by Harris & Fink (1987) revealed that recruiter competence was significantly related to regard for company by employees. Chapman et al. (2005) found that recruiter competence was related to applicant's attraction towards organization. Fisher et al. (1979) theorized that, organizational recruiters would be short of reliability in comparison to the other employees of the organization. The base of their (Fisher et al., 1979) contention is based on the assumption that organizational recruiters would be seen by candidates as deficient in proficiency relating to what a job entails and would be perceived as having a vested interest in filling vacancies. Researchers (e.g., Maurer, Howe, & Lee, 1992) also have theorized that credibility of recruiter is helpful in explaining the differential impact of recruiters on candidates.

Work experience of the applicants' has been projected as a negative moderator of the effectiveness of the recruitment-reactions relationship. Those applicants who have greater work experience are expected to be aware of the fact that while working job attributes are more important in influencing satisfaction than other recruitment elements experienced at the time of searching a job (Rynes et al., 1980). Liden & Parsons (1986) and Harris & Fink (1987) examined recruiter gender and suggested that the recruiter's personableness, as well as how informative he or she was, influenced the applicants affect toward the job, not the gender of the recruiter. During an interaction with female or minority recruiters, it may indicate to the candidate that an employer values diversity in organization. This kind of value system may make a job more interesting to certain job applicants (Highhouse, Stierwalt, Bachiochi, Elder, & Fisher, 1999).

Though, researchers have hypothesized about the positive impressions of recruiters who are well informed, trustworthy, amiable, and demographically diverse, researchers have not paid much attention on the fundamental reasons as to why different recruiters may influence the attention prospective applicants give to a job opening or the interest they show in a position. Schmitt and Coyle (1976) contend that not only does the applicant draw conclusions about the job and organization from the recruiter, but also that the recruiter's characteristics and presentation are related to the likelihood of the applicant accepting employment. After considering the importance of attracting attention of the applicants and creating their interest, undoubtedly these two issues worth future attention.

To sum up, it can be strongly said that the choice of a recruiter make a difference (Rynes et al., 1991).

2.4.3 Interview Structure

The interview is considered as a recruitment tool that can provide job information to the candidate and helps interviewer present her/his organization with an intention to attract the "right" candidates and convince candidates to accept a job offer (Alderfer and McCord, 1970; Schmitt, 1976; Schmitt and Coyle, 1976). Employment interviews are considered as both recruitment and selection tools. Rynes (1988) takes into consideration the repercussions of viewing the interview from recruitment point of view rather than a selection perspective. Arvey and Champion (1982) speculated that employers may rely on interview to sell applicants on the job, to respond to applicant questions, and to serve as a public relations tool. Jablin and McComb (1984) and Herriot (1988, 1989) proposed that the interview should be considered as an information, expectation and perception exchange event.

Webster defines interview as a "meeting of people face to face to confer about something." Within the human resource context Meyers (1992) describes the interview as an activity that involves asking a set of questions to help the interviewer make a sound hiring decision. Similarly Connerley and Rynes (1997) view that in most of the screening focused interviews; there is likelihood of recruiters to ask more difficult questions than in attraction based interviews. In attraction based interviews the recruiter give more attention to 'selling' the organization and vacancy to the candidates.

Schmitt and Coyle (1976) contend that the interviewer's empathetic behaviour, preparation, and ability to supply information together predict applicant's perception of his/her performance and the extent of favourability towards an organization. They have further suggested that the interviewer's personality, delivery style (Schmitt and Coyle, 1976) and the sufficiency of the job information (Barber et al., 1994) forecast candidates' decisions. When interviewers show importance in interviewees, it has been found to be more satisfied; it gives interviewees the chance to show their technical knowledge, talk about the job profile and organization, and analyse the career development of employees similar to the candidates (Alderfer and McCord, 1970; Keenan and Wedderburn, 1980).

Those interviewers who confer more importance to the recruitment give the candidate more precise knowledge about the organization's post-interview decision processes, and commence earlier contacts followed by the interview (Hanigan, 1987). Alternatively Harn and Thornton (1985), Harris & Fink (1985), and Powell (1991) did not come across the issue that the interviewer's informativeness has any considerable main effect on interviewees' judgments. A study by Liden & Parsons (1986) contended that females viewed interviewers as more competent and personable to them. According to Rynes (1988) with increasing importance of the recruitment function, employment interviewers are assumed to: (1) show more affirmative verbal and nonverbal behaviours, (2) give more importance to vacancy rather than applicant characteristics; (3) illustrate vacancies in more favourable terms, (4) ask questions that are less prone to result in candidate disqualification, and (5) follow rigorous post-interview follow up policies.

A model of interviewer effectiveness proposed by Graves (1993) suggests that effective interviewers use more positive nonverbal behaviours. Study by Papadopoulou et al. (1996) depict that the level of empathy shown by the interviewer towards interviewee influenced their perceptions of the interviewer's competence as a provider of important information and his/her readiness to let the applicants to present themselves effectively. It is seen while exploring the applicants' contentment with the interviewer; it came into sight that the interviewees were more pleased with interviewer's capability to control the interview. The candidates perceived that an affectionate, sensitive and helpful interviewer as willing and/or competent to give the applicants information related to the job and the company, than an apathetic and inconsiderate interviewer. The participants of this study did not show to be influenced by the empathy of the interviewer in their choices. Thus, for effective interviewing Huffcutt and Woehr (1999) suggested that (1) training should be provided to interviewers regardless of whether the interview itself (i.e. the questions and rating scales) is structured (2) the same interviewer should be used across all applicants, especially when the interview itself is not highly structured; and (3) using a panel of interviewers does not contribute to validity.

The structure of the recruiting interview can influence whether and how easily a job seeker can get needed information. Campion et al. (1998) defined interview structure as any enhancement that increases standardization or otherwise assists the interviewer in determining what questions to ask or how to evaluate the responses. Some recruiting interviews are dual-purpose in that they combine recruitment with preliminary employee selection. In the 80 years of published research on employment interviews, one of the most strongly supported conclusions is that structuring the interview enhances its reliability and validity and, hence, its usefulness for prediction and decision making (Campion et al., 1998).

Fifteen components of structure are identified by Campion et al. (1997) that may improve either the components of the interview or the process of evaluation in the interview. Hyde (1997) conducted a study of job applicants' participation in employment interviews, which suggested that attention to the structure of interviews could enhance their recruitment value. Her results indicated that applicants perceive interview more favourably when the applicant had an opportunity to ask question, when interviewer questions were not situational, and when the interviewer was knowledgeable about the applicant's resume. Similarly, Rynes and Connerley (1993) found that applicants viewed tough interview questions positively, so as they were job-related.

While explaining structure of interview Campion et al. (1997, 1998) gave various suggestions like the questions during interview should be based on a job analysis, same questions should be asked to all candidates, interviewer should limit probing and follow up questioning and elaboration on questions, questions should be structured and specific, interviewer should spend enough time with candidate and ask sufficient number of questions to them, he should be able to withhold or control ancillary information, and finally he should not allow uncontrolled questions from candidate until after the interview.

Dibble (1999) pointed out that potential employees should be treated as if they are prospective customers during their interviewing phase, as they have the command and knowledge of their abilities and they trust on their worth in the marketplace. The most awful mistake that a company can make is to fake its culture, reward system, advancement/development possibilities and/or business strategy (Kreisman, 2002). Carefully developed structured employment interviews have been found to predict turnover with a corrected correlation of 0.39 (Schmidt & Rader, 1999).

However, all research studies mentioned above did not explain applicants' reaction to interview process and also its long term relationship with employee behaviour (Taylor & Bergmann, 1987).

2.4.4 Applicant Attractors

Organizations are all the time been worried about attracting and selecting the right types of employees (Schneider, 1976, 1987). The study related to applicant attraction is termed differently by different authors. Various terms used are job inducements, job attractors, applicant attractors, attraction inducements, etc.

Efficiency wage theory (Weiss, 1980; Yellen, 1984) proposes that choice to increase attraction inducements have a positive influence on the quality, as well as quantity, of the pool of candidates drowned and retained by organizations. The use of benefits as a recruiting device is prevalent in labour and personnel economics. In a similar vein, Rosen's (1986) work on 'equalizing differences' establishes a theory for how non-wage benefits affect the composition of workers attracted to a firm. Attraction related theories and research are scattered across a variety of literatures, and often are identified with other topics like wage, motivation, or discrimination theories (Rynes & Barber, 1990).

Various organizational attributes such as training, compensation and advancement opportunities have been seen to have positive effects on applicant attraction to firms (Powell, 1984; Taylor & Bergmann, 1987). Recruitment researchers have started to understand as to how various organizational factors other than recruitment practices can influence recruitment outcomes. The goal of organizations is not only to attract employees, but to also attract those who would stay as a result of the initial organizational attractiveness. Even though the organisational attraction study has exposed some insights, still there is much to be learned (Barber 1998).

In a term job inducements, word 'inducements' express the idea of intentionally modifying attributes for the precise purpose of increasing the attractiveness of a job to potential candidates (Rynes & Barber, 1990). Various studies (Rynes, 1991; Gatewood, Gowan, & Lautenschlager, 1993) advocate that early recruitment practices, corporate advertising, and reputation may all influence recruitment outcomes by affecting candidates' perceptions and decisions to apply during the early stage of recruitment. The efficiency of different recruitment strategies may limit or enhance due to prior exposure to a company through various organizational factors (Rynes, Bretz, & Gerhart, 1991). Similarly, Gatewood et. al. (1993) found the decision of candidate to pursue employment with the company is perceived by the organisation's image.

A great deal of research suggests that job and organization attributes play an important role in job pursuit and decisions, and that more information about job and organization attributes during recruitment is related to attraction (Rynes, Bretz, & Gerhart, 1991; Barber, 1998; Allen et al., 2004). As mentioned by Marcus Buckingham and Curt Coffman (1999) in their recent book, "First Break All the Rules", a talented employee *"may join a company because of its charismatic leaders, its generous benefits, and its world class training programs, but how long that employee stays and how productive he is while there is determined by his relationship with his immediate supervisor".*

Cable and Turban (2001) saw to theory and research on marketing brand equity to design an extensive model of how firms persuade the decision making of job seekers. Specifically, they pointed that corporate advertising and firm reputation are expected to have an effect on job seekers by affecting their awareness and perceptions of an organization. The most effective strategies for attracting and keeping the best people within organizations are to continue giving individuals reasons to select that organization as the place to work. This includes paying attention to the work environment, the employees' future within the company, the pay they receive as well as the rewards available for their efforts and contributions made (RCI Resource Centre, 2001).

Collins and Stevens (2002) in their conclusions recommended that companies may follow variety of recruitment strategies in order to attract applicants. A strong employer brand attracts better applicants (Collins & Stevens 2002, Slaughter et al. 2004) and shapes their expectations about their employment (Livens & Highhouse 2003). Adamsky (2005) outlines ways the recruiters can support in building a better organisation branding: they are, employment branding – gaining and marketing a reputation for being a good employer – allows to more easily hiring the candidates; aggressively pursuing top talent and attracting them to your organisation; creating better employee referral programmes so that employees support the HR; looking at talent as opposed to workforce planning and investing in employees.

A study by Collen Flaherty (2007) shows that benefits like tuition reimbursement programs affect the type of workers attracted to the firm and the retention rates of employees. Amundson (2007) has recognized 10 attractor factors that appear to play important roles with respect to employee attraction. Those factors are job security, location, relationships, recognition, contribution, work fit, flexibility, learning, responsibility, and innovation.

Attention must be paid to both the residual effects of recruitment campaigns and the cost of marketing in building company branding. A few models emphasize that the effects of attraction strategies may spill over beyond the job choice decisions of current applicants (e.g., Rynes et al., 1980). Both theoretical and empirical works have suggested that variations in attraction practices can have important effects on long-term (i.e., post-acceptance) outcomes as well. For example, organization applicant interactions may influence applicants' subsequent decisions to stay committed or leave the organization. Decisions to enhance attraction inducements (e.g., housing assistance, higher starting salaries) have been shown to lead to reduced turnover (Hamlet, 1989; Lakhani, 1988). Turban and Cable (2003) established positive connections between organization reputation and organization-level recruitment outcomes.

Thus, it becomes essential to understand the role of applicant attractors along with other recruitment strategy variables in gaining post hire outcomes to the organization.

2.4.5 Source of Recruitment

The important question that an organization needs to tackle in trying to fill job openings is how to approach individuals who may be qualified for and interested in the job openings of organization. There are numerous sources that make up the recruiting process. The right human-capital management system would allow us to measure both internal and external resources. Organizations use variety of methods to recruit job candidates, like advertising through various media, employee referrals, and employment agencies, walk-ins. Kirnan et al. (1989) depicts that previous research has divided recruiting source into two general categories: formal recruiting sources (viz. public and private employment agencies, trade unions, school or college placement bureaus, and advertisements through radio, television, newspapers, or professional journals) and informal recruiting sources (consisting primarily of employee referrals, referrals by friends or relatives, and self-initiated applications such as walk-ins and write-ins).

While Fisher et al. (2005) contend that candidates can be recruited from either internal source or external sources. In internal sources are promotion and transfer of existing employees, and recommendations from the internal employees of the organization. While external sources are mail applicants, application file, employment exchanges, agencies and consultants, professional associations, and educational institutes etc.

Since many years, various researchers have examined the utility of different recruitment sources and whether certain sources are associated to useful outcomes. Evaluating the effectiveness of an organization's recruiting efforts may involve an analysis of the relationship between the sources of recruitment and relevant organizational criteria (Quaglieri, 1982). According to Schwab (1982) some methods are likely to be more effective (in terms of yielding lower post-hire rates of turnover and absenteeism and higher levels of job performance) simply because they provide more information on which to base selection decisions. To add, recruitment sources vary in effectiveness because they reach applicants from different populations.

Many research studies have showed that informal recruiting sources lead to superior new hires compared to candidates recruited through formal sources (Gannon, 1971; Decker & Cornelius, 1979; Breaugh, 1981). Quaglieri (1982) revealed that newly hired candidates consider informal sources as more specific and more accurate in their portrayals of the job than formal sources. Kirnan (1986) contended that informal sources of recruitment (five different types of referrals) had superior survival rates than formal sources of recruitment (employment agencies, newspaper advertisements, and school placement). Aamodt and Carr (1988) studied recruitment source differences for tenure, where the employee referrals have the longest tenure followed by walk-ins, employment agencies, and ads. Kirnan, Farley, and Geisinger (1989) contended that employees recruited via informal sources (e.g., employee referrals) were of higher quality and there were more chances of job offers to them. Williams, Labig, and Stone (1993) also concluded that informal sources of recruitment get in touch with differently qualified applicants, which, in turn, were strong predictors of successive employee performance. Almost half of employees view referring people to the company a good thing, as it both gives them a chance to help a friend and gives them the opportunity to work with people they know, trust, and respect. The employee referral mechanism also encourages employees to contribute to the shape of the company and leads to employees who are prone to stay.

Newly employed candidates recruited via internal recruitment sources are assumed to have more information about the organization than employees recruited via external recruitment sources before joining the organization. The employees who are recruited through walk-ins come under third remaining group, and it does not present clear proof on the type of information these candidates have before joining the organization. Wanous (1992) contended that recruitment of employees through internal recruitment sources leads to slightly higher job survival rate than recruiting through external sources of recruitment.

Various studies are conducted to find source effectiveness. Most of them have measured effectiveness in terms of survival rate, rate of turnover, performance, and commitment to the organization. A study by Ullman (1966) was one of the initial studies which examined recruitment sources. His results showed that newly employed candidates who were recruited via informal sources (i.e., employee referrals, direct applications) had a lower rate of turnover than employees recruited via formal sources (i.e., newspaper advertisements, employment agencies). Gannon (1971) examined the relationship of the sources of employee referral in the recruitment effort and the amount of turnover in the organization. Results suggest that referrals such as rehiring of a former employee, the hiring of an individual with a reference from his or her high school or by a present employee, are successful predictors of stable employees. In addition, results suggest that despite the limitations of the research (e.g. demographics, attitude of employees), employee turnover could be reduced through an examination of the procedures that are successful in attracting and maintaining applicants. Decker and Cornelius (1979), Taylor and Schmidt (1983), and Saks (1994) got similar to the results of Gannon. Results by Taylor (1983) further showed that the rehire source was found to yield employees having significantly longer tenure than those recruited from television, newspaper, and the public employment service. Latham and Leddy (1987) reported that employees recruited through employee referral are more satisfied with their job and show higher organizational commitment as compared to the candidates recruited through newspaper advertisements. Few more studies have found employee referrals and other informal recruitment sources generate positive outcomes (Breaugh, 1981; Kirman, Farley, & Geisinger, 1989). Employee referrals had higher retention rate than those recruited from newspaper ads (Breaugh & Mann, 1984). Conard and Ashworth (1986) evaluated employee referrals and newspaper advertisements, and came to the conclusion that employee referrals had higher job survival rates. An Ohio State University study, for instance, shows that employees hired through referrals are 25 percent more likely to stay with the company than employees hired through other methods. Williams, Labig and Stone (1993) contend that source of recruitment was inversely related to voluntary turnover after one year.

Some literature on effective recruitment method shows that newspaper ads tend to be associated with higher rates of turnover and poorer employee performance (Schwab, 1982). Individuals recruited via certain sources (e.g. newspapers, employment agencies) may have unrealistically high expectations of what the job entails. Decker and Cornelius (1979) contemplated that employees recruited via newspaper advertisements or employment agencies might be more inclined to leave the organization because they possess more knowledge of job possibilities. Newspaper is the source that helps in appealing those who are looking for a job - active job seekers. Newspaper ads need to be assisted with other sources to attract other passive job seekers. Breaugh (1981) found little evidence for the case that those recruited through newspaper advertisements lost almost twice as many work days as those recruited via other sources.

In contrast to above studies there are few studies showing no significant association or correlation of source and organizational outcome. A study by Swaroff, Barclay, and Bass (1985) failed to find recruitment source as having a significant effect on turnover. Williams, Labig, and Stone (1993) were unable to find any recruitment source effects on employee turnover or job performance. Saks (1994) established that in case of seasonal employees, those recruited through informal recruitment sources (rehires, employee referral, self-initiated walk-ins) when compared with those recruited through formal recruitment sources (newspaper advertisement, radio advertisement, poster) showed no difference in commitment level towards organization. Barber (1998) after reviewing the research on recruitment sources concluded that past research does not make any strong case for the importance of recruitment source differences.

Breaugh (1981) found no considerable differentiations between employees recruited via four recruitment sources on several demographic variables viz. age, education, sex, and tenure with the organization, years in current position, and tenure with current supervisor. On the contrary, Taylor & Schmidt (1983) came across source differences for age, sex, shift preference, and previous pay. Nevertheless, it is pointed that there were no significant distinction on these variables for the employees recruited via: television, radio, newspaper, employee referral, direct applications and public employment agency (Breaugh & Mann, 1984). They further found that employees recruited via newspaper advertisements were more likely to be male and older. Swaroff et al. (1985) contended that employees recruited via newspaper advertisements are be likely to be older than those recruited via employee referrals, employment agencies, or college recruiting. Werbel and Landau (1996) further depicted that employees recruited via employer contact were older than employees recruited via college placement programs, and that employee referrals were less educated than college placement recruits. Griffeth et al. (1997) investigated a array of demographic differences across sources; these differences are not related to the differences in outcomes, thus showing only little support for the explanation related to individual differences.

In a nutshell, in order to improve knowledge on recruitment source effectiveness further study needs to be conducted. Ideally, each firm should conduct its own analysis of source quality for each type of job. Recruiting sources that are of low quality can be used less intensively or eliminated altogether in future recruiting (Fisher et al., 2005). Although previous research has documented important recruitment source differences (e.g., performance, turnover), the reason for these differences is not entirely clear. Research more theoretical in nature is required to understand the cause of source differences.

The important concept emerging from all the above recruitment strategy variables related studies is that recruitment strategy exhibit differential effectiveness and therefore it may be utilized as indicators in order to establish the most effective strategy, relevant to the organization. As per literature all these variables individually lead to certain post hire outcomes like commitment, burnout, or turnover. It will be interesting to understand if these variables show same results in different occupational and cultural context? And also if these variables together have same effect on the outcome variables?

2.5 Employee Retention Variables

Retention is nothing but stopping people from leaving organization or keeping good people. The retention of quality employees is important for three important and basic reasons: 1) the increasing importance of intellectual capital; 2) a causal link between employee tenure and customer satisfaction; and 3) the high cost of employee turnover (Harvard Business Essentials, 2002).

Retention can be categorized as functional or dysfunctional and avoidable or unavoidable. (Dalton et al., 1982; Woods and Macauly, 1989; Johnson, Griffeth, and Griffin, 2000). Retention is recognized as functional when non-performers leave and performers stay and can in fact assist organizations to improve its performance (Johnson et al., 2000). As oppose to this, when performers leave and non-performers stay, retention is highly dysfunctional, and it hampers organizational innovation and performance (Abbasi & Hollman, 2000). While *unavoidable turnover* occurs when an organization has no control over the reasons for an employee's exit (e.g. spouse's relocation) and *avoidable turnover* takes place when employees leave a company for better pay, better working conditions, etc. (Dalton et al., 1982; Woods and Macauly, 1989).

When individual components of commitment, job satisfaction, satisfaction with pay, promotion, supervision, co-workers, and the work itself have been studied, fairly consistent relationships have been found with the propensity to remain (Friedlander & Walton, 1964; Knowles, 1964; Ley, 1966; Hulin, 1968; Farris, 1971; Susskind et al. 2000). There are few studies that recommend retention programs which help reduce turnover and its effects. Boles et al. (1995) recommended that if the intention is to reduce employee turnover, the organization should use of pre-employment applicant demographics. Other factors like realistic job previews, job enrichment, workspace characteristics or socialization practices are part of retention activities (Pizam and Ellis, 1999). As an attempt to search and retain employees, many organizations make use of incentives such as pay, benefits, promotions, and training. Still, such attempts often tend to ignore their goal, as a few research studies pointed that the front line manger is the key to attracting and retaining employees (Buckingham and Coffman, 1999). A Ph.D. study by Jernigan (2008) showed that retention decisions of nurses are related to factors external to the leader /superior subordinate relationship. Different aspect of retention is focused by Muhammad (1990) who found that stressors, such as work overload and role ambiguity, might cause the employee to have low job satisfaction and motivation, subsequently resulting in low organizational commitment, burnout and high turnover.

Many other studies show that variety of factors affect retention in the organizations. Like, companies with better organization culture show better retention rates (Sheridan, 1992; Deery and Shaw, 1999). Kaak et al. (1997) explored the concept of turnover culture among non-supervisory hotel employees. You (1998) explored the role of candidate's nationality in forecasting their turnover behaviour in the US and South Korea. IDS Management Review (2000) as mentioned in Newman et. al. (2002) contends that the foundation of an effective retention strategy is reliable information on the level of turnover and an understanding of its causes. Few studies attempted to find such relationships between other variables and retention. Like, Susskind et al. (2000) proposed that perceived organizational support influence organizational commitment to the greater extent. Lee and Chon (2000) investigated the influence of employee diversity on turnover in the restaurant industry. Mak and Sokel, (2001) suggested to improve retention, the company should adopt career development policies in alignment with the needs of the employees. Newman, Maylor & Chansarkar (2002) found out five main perceptions of retention strategies. They are (as per rank) better working conditions (more staffing and resources), more pay, better management, improved opportunities for training and better career prospects. While the results of study by Mattox and Jinkerson (2005) indicated that training had a positive impact on retention rates and thus the length of time employees stay.

Thus, retention is nothing but people staying with an organization. And there are three types of people staying in the organization. They are; employees committed to the organization, people with turnover intent who are ready to leave the organization as soon as possible, and burnouts, who experience a type of prolonged occupational stress. It is seen in the literature that lack of commitment leads to higher level of burnout and turnover intentions, and burnout also leads to turnover intent among employees. The same relationship can be explained considering studies by various researchers.

When employees feel committed to the organization they are likely to stay in the organization. Consequences of burnout (work exhaustion) include reduced organizational commitment (Jackson, Turner, and Brief, 1987; Leiter, and Maslach, 1988; Leiter, 1991; Leiter, Clark, and Durup, 1994; Thomas, and Williams, 1995). Burnout has been constantly studies in relation to the withdrawal intentions, leading to withdrawal behaviours, or coping mechanisms, such as diminished commitment, depersonalization, and ultimately voluntary turnover. Using human resources service professionals as the research participants Kahill (1988), in a longitudinal study, found that burnout negatively affected job involvement and organizational commitment.

Burnout, or work exhaustion has come out to be a strong aspect that existing research has continually revealed to be correlated to work attitudes e.g. job satisfaction, organizational commitment, and turnover intention. Consequences of burnout include higher turnover intention (Jackson, Turner, and Brief, 1987; Thomas, and Williams, 1995; Firth, and Britton, 1989; Jackson, Schwab, and Schuler, 1986; Lee, and Ashforth, 1993; Maslach, and Jackson, 1984a; Maslach, and Jackson, 1984b). Ellen Moore (2000) investigated work exhaustion as a possible mediating factor of turnover intention. Dan Ray has found that there is positive relationship between burnout and turnover intent (Dany Ray, 2003). Larson too contends that burnout is positively related to turnover intention.

Jaros (1997) showed concern to the fact that, the relationship between organizational commitment and turnover intention may not be as simple as is projected in several turnover models. Numerous studies involving voluntary turnover in organizations has considered organizational commitment as an important construct. Overall, empirical tests over and over again support the significant negative relationships between organizational commitment and turnover intention (Steers, 1977; Angle and Perry, 1981; Mathieu & Zajac, 1990; Irving, Coleman, & Cooper, 1997; Susskind et al., 2000; Griffeth et al., 2000; Labatmediene et al., 2007). Thus, it can be said that commitment is negatively related to turnover intention. Study that looked at both satisfaction and commitment found them to have a similar strength of association with turnover intentions (Parasuraman 1989). In contrast to that Tett & Meyer (1993) contend that intention/ cognitions are predicted more strongly by satisfaction than by commitment. Similarly, results by Ahuja et. al. (2002) shows that low levels of job satisfaction and organizational commitment affect turnover intention for virtual workers. Study by Shahnawaz and Jafri in the Indian context showed similar results that there is significant correlation between organizational commitment and turnover intent. Elangovan (2001) has contended that there is a reciprocal link between organizational commitment and turnover intention, i.e. low level of commitment leads to increase in turnover intention, which in turn lowers commitment. Study by Karsh, Booske and Sainfort (2005) concluded that organizational identification (i.e. commitment) and both intrinsic and extrinsic satisfaction were significant predictors of intentions to stay.

It further becomes essential to understand these categories (Loyals, Burnout, Turnover Intent) of people so that their relationship with recruitment strategy variable can be studied effectively.

2.5.1 Commitment

The decision to remain with an organization is largely determined by an employee's level of commitment to the organization (Miller, 1996). Organisational commitment is described as an employees' identification and involvement with the organization, which includes agreeing to the organisational goals and values, keenness to work hard, and intention to remain with the organization (Crewson 1997). Wiener (1982) defined commitment as the 'totality of internalized normative pressures to act in a way which meets organizational goals and interests', and suggests that individuals exhibit behaviours solely because 'they believe it is the "right" and moral thing to do' (p. 421). Loyal, engaged employees are inclined to produce high performance business outcomes that can be measured by increase in the sales, improvement in the productivity, profitability and superior employee retention (Tsui et. al. 1995; Rogers 2001).

Age, sex, race, personality, attitudes, climate, and culture are few factors that can influence organizational commitment (Steers, 1977); and values, fairness of policies, decentralization, competence, job challenges, degree of autonomy, and variety of skills used (Meyer & Allen, 1997). It is also found that in case of dearth of quality job alternatives, strong commitment towards job is seen (Rusbult & Farrell, 1983). There is some evidence seen by Cohen & Gattiker (1994) that even pay attitudes are related to commitment and quit intentions. Non-work variables that are considered for the study involves family, hobbies, religion, political influences that can influence job attitudes (Cohen, 1995; Mitchell et al., 2001; Rouse, 2001). As stated by Sayeed (2001) in his book, that a positive, yet less desirable, outcome arising from non-commitment (positive in terms of the individual's continued growth and development but less desirable from the organization's point of view) is that employees seek better employment opportunities elsewhere which leads to turnover. A study by Priyadarshi (2011) found compensation and career facet of the employer brand attributes to be negatively related to organizational commitment.

Extensive literature on commitment has happened. In most of the studies attention has been directed toward organizational commitment as the attitudinal component of organizational relevant behaviour (Hrebiniak and Alutto, 1972; Buchanan, 1974; Porter et al., 1974; Porter, Crampon and Smith, 1976; Steers, 1977a; Stevens, Beyer and Trice, 1978). Few researchers have proposed that the concept of commitment may disclose reliable linkages between attitudes and behaviour, because commitment is presumed to be a relatively stable employee attribute (Porter et al., 1974; Koch and Steers, 1978).

Researchers have explored different types or bases of commitment to an organization. Major studies in the area of organizational commitment leading to development of measurement scale can be explained briefly as follows:

Organizational Commitment Questionnaire (OCQ)

Porter et al. (1974) defined organizational commitment in terms of the strength of an individual's identification with and involvement in a particular organization. Such commitment can normally be characterized by three factors: (a) a strong belief in and acceptance of the organization's goals and values; *(b)* a willingness to exert considerable effort on behalf of the organization; *(c)* a definite desire to maintain organizational membership. Porter et al. constructed a 15-item instrument to measure employees' satisfaction and level of involvement in the organization.

Balaji (1986)

Balaji (1986) attempted to develop an organizational commitment scale suited to Indian organizational environment. However, his effort suffered from a few shortcomings. First, the items were relevant but failed to fully encompass the organizational commitment construct because of brevity of length. Second, some items have apparently been picked up from the organizational commitment scale of Mowdy et al. (1982) instead of building up a scale based on the Indian organizational psyche, in general and a systematic analysis of the organizational behaviour literature, in particular.

Organizational Commitment (OC)

O'Reilly and Chatman (1986) suggested three different types of psychological bonds viz. compliance, identification, and internalization provides the basis for commitment. The OCQ has two versions. O'Reilly and Chatman (1986) and Reichers (1985) criticized the original 15-item version because of the overlap of some items with the concept they are supposed to predict, turnover. This criticism has led some researchers to use a shorter version of the OCQ that omits the problematic items (Aaron Cohen, 1993).

Meyer and Allen (1991)

Meyer and Allen (1991) distinguished between continuance, affective, and normative types of commitment. Employees with strong affective commitment remain because they *want* to, those with strong continuance commitment because they *need to*, and those with strong normative commitment because they feel they *ought* to do so. This model is the most frequently used organizational commitment scale as can be seen its prevalence in today's literature. According to Meyer and Allen (1991) scale of organizational commitment, employees would remain with their organization on the basis of their positive feelings, emotion and attachment to the organization, which is quite like to the element of organizational fit.

Attitudinal or affective commitment is in general well-suited with the vital orientation in the organizational behaviour literature that studies commitment as reflection of an individual's psychological attachment to an organization (Porter, Steers, Mowday, & Boulian, 1974; Meyer & Allen, 1991). That attachment may be to other individuals in the organization (affiliation), to the organization as an entity (identification), or to its mission and/or values (internalization). Continuance commitment involves the recognition of costs associated with leaving the organization. Two sub-dimensions of continuance commitment; personal sacrifice and lack of alternatives have been identified in an analysis of the construct definition of commitment (Dunham et al. 1994). It reflects a "side bets theory" (Becker, 1960) in which employees will maintain their membership in an organization if their personal investment in that organization is greater than the advantages of leaving. The normative component is commitment based on feelings of obligation. It is similar to the peer pressure in which there is a feeling of obligation of the employee to stay with the organization.

Balfour and Wechsler (1994) identified the three dimensions of exchange, affiliation, and identification commitment. Wilson and Laschinger (1994) found that access to information, support, resources, and opportunities were all significantly correlated with organizational commitment, as were age and tenure.

Individual factors influencing employee commitment are age, gender, tenure and education. The same can be explained in detail as follows:

Literature (Cohen & Lowenberg, 1990; Matthieu & Zajac, 1990), argues that, in general, the relations of organizational commitment with age and with tenure have produced few large correlations. Age was suggested as the best indicators of organizational commitment (Becker, 1960; Meyer & Allen, 1984; Sheldon, 1971; Labatmediene et al. (2007)). Angel & Perry (1981) also contend that age was one of the positive correlates of commitment. As per the finding by Cohen (1993) the relation between organizational commitment and age was strongest for the youngest subgroup. While Cohen (1993) contends that the relation between organizational commitment and tenure was strongest for the oldest tenure subgroup.

Gender is one of the most popular demographic variables in commitment studies. Some researchers (Singh et al., 2004; Savery and Syme, 1996) contend that men are more committed to the organization than women; while others (Powell, in Singh et al., 2004) do not find gender differences. Contrary to these results, Angel & Perry (1981), Singh et al. (2004), Marchiori and Henkin (2004) and Dixon et al. (2005) have found that women have higher levels of organizational commitment. The rationale usually presented for such findings is that females enjoy less interorganizational mobility than males and, therefore, tend to become restricted to their present organizations.

Becker (1960) argues that an employee's investment of time and effort makes it more difficult to leave the organization; the more time with the organization, the more investments. Meyer and Allen (1984) argued that younger employees show more commitment because of their awareness that they will have less job opportunities if they leave current organization with less work experience. As they gain experience more job opportunities will be available. Metcalfe and Dick (2000) found support for the proposition that organisational commitment increases with length of tenure. Similar results are found by Lok and Crawford (2001) in a multiple regression that tenure, was statistically (negatively) significant in explaining organizational commitment variance.

Findings by various researchers (Angel & Perry 1981; Sheldon, 1971; Hrebiniakand Alutto, 1972; Steers, 1977a; Stevens, Beyer, and Trice, 1978) show that commitment was negatively related to educational level. The argument often used to explain these relationships is that decreasing levels of education tend to reduce the feasibility of obtaining desirable alternative job and therefore tend to restrict the individual to the present organization.

The reason that commitment has received so much attention is that it has been found to predict turnover intentions (e.g. Martin 1982, Francis-Felsen et al. 1996).

2.5.2 Burnout

Burnout can straightforwardly hamper company's retention activities and if the organization develops a status as a burnout chamber, it will have trouble hiring good people (Harvard business essentials, 2002). Maslach (1976) defined burnout as "a syndrome of emotional exhaustion and cynicism that frequently occurs among people who do 'people work'...who spend considerable time in close encounters". In the research literature, burnout or also called as work exhaustion was primarily covered by the construct of tedium, which is defined as a situation of physical, emotional, and mental exhaustion, where mental exhaustion is due to by long-term involvement in challenging work set-up (Pines et al.1981). Maslach & Jackson (1981) define burnout as a psychological syndrome of emotional exhaustion, depersonalization (callous or negative behaviour towards others) and diminished personal accomplishment that occurs among individuals who work in human service. Gillian Walker (1986) argues that "burnout" is no mere concept, a "thing" or syndrome but is a moment in a social relation which provides for and is a social course of action. Cordes and Dougherty (1993) attempted to generalize burnout in the context of corporate and industrial environments. Schaufeli and Enzmann (1998) defined burnout as "a special type of prolonged occupational stress that results particularly from interpersonal demands at work" and Cooper et al. (2001) as "caused by chronic job stress".

Burnout is often studied within the frame of stress research. Pines and Keinan (2005) contend that job importance (assumed to be intervening variable) was more highly correlated with burnout. Similarly, other antecedents to exhaustion receiving consistent empirical support include work overload (e.g., Jackson et al. 1986, 1987; Lieter 1991; Pines et al. 1981); role conflict and role ambiguity (e.g., Burke and Greenglass 1995; Fimian and Blanton 1987; Jackson et al. 1986; Pines et al. 1981; Sethi et al. 1999); lack of autonomy (e.g., Jackson et al. 1986; Landsbergis 1988; Pines et al. 1981); and lack of rewards (e.g., Jackson et al. 1986; Pines et al. 1981).

Researchers contend that the causes of burnout can be unrealistic expectations, perfectionism or over idealism in relation to reality on the part of the individual (Freudenberger, 1975; 1980; Vash, 1980; Giuffra, 1981). In a study of 66 managers, feeling overextended was not correlated with burnout, but it was significantly correlated with having influence (Kafry & Pines, 1980). The prominent burnout researcher Ayala Pines (1993) suggested that burnout can be understood as an instance in which one's important work-related goals are frustrated and blocked by circumstances that cause failure. Tewari and Tiwari (1995) studied the relationship between burnout and total control as one of the factors in organisational climate in the Indian nationalised and scheduled banks. The study showed that compared to the employees of nationalised banks, the employees of scheduled banks showed significantly higher emotional exhaustion and lower feeling of personal accomplishment.

Pines (2000) revealed that certain work facets that correlate with burnout are likely to be those that offer employees with a sense of importance. Thus, in a study on 100 hospital nurses the burnout was not correlated with the number of hours they worked but it was significantly correlated with their feeling of accomplishment. In contrast, no significant correlation between autonomy given to employee and work exhaustion seen in a study conducted by Moore's (2000). Study by Sharma (2002) reveals that role overload and self-role distance are critical determinants of burnout among Indian executives. Role overload has emerged as more powerful determinant of burnout as it can predict both depersonalization and emotional exhaustion. Similarly, people, who give higher importance to their sense of existential significance in their work, select their careers with high objectives and expectations, and are optimistic and motivated. The time when they feel that they are unsuccessful, that their work is not worth mentioning, that they make no difference in the world, they start feeling helpless and loose hope and in the end burn out (Malach, Pines, Keinan, 2005). Study by Pines & Keinen (2005) contends that the work importance was more highly correlated with burnout than with strain. Burnout was also more highly correlated with other variables such as lack of job satisfaction, a desire to quit the job, physical and emotional symptoms and perceived performance level.

Various models developed by researchers can be explained briefly as follows:

Veninga and Spradley's Stage Model

According to Veninga and Spradley (1981) that burnout developed in the form of five different stages:

Honeymoon stage: This stage is portrayed by the feelings of excitement, enthusiasm, pride, and challenge due to the excitement involved in the new job. This leads to certain coping mechanisms and strategies, which show to be dysfunctional afterward. This also has a flip side that it shows the start of the depletion of energy.

Fuel shortage stage: In this stage future difficulties like general, undefined feelings of fatigue, sleep disturbance, inefficiency, and job dissatisfaction are indicated. Such interruptions, in turn, can result in concurrent behaviours of increased eating, drinking, and smoking.

Chronic symptom stage: At this stage the physiological symptoms from previous stage becomes more prominent and gets heightened and might even lead to the incidents of indicators like physical illnesses, anger, irritation, and depression.

Crisis stage: After certain time duration, the symptoms may develop into acute psychosomatic disorders like peptic ulcer, tension headache, chronic backache, high blood pressure; sleep disturbance, etc., along with the growth of various means to escape to face the increasing behaviours of self doubt, a pessimistic view of life, and a general feeling of oppression.

Hitting the wall stage: At this final stage, an individual is stressed due to his inability to cope with stress. The model recommended by Veninga and Spradley (1981) is indicative in imagery and could lend a hand to a person to identify the warning signals and take preventive actions but it is difficult to design a rigorous analytical model.

Maslach Model 1981

Maslach and Jackson (1981) theorized burnout as a syndrome consisting of three elements. First, *Emotional exhaustion* shows a mental and physical tension and strain due to job-related factors. Second, *Depersonalization* is a keeping oneself away from others and looking at others impersonally. This is a kind of reaction to the chronic emotional strain of dealing at length with other human beings, especially when they are bothered or are having problems. *Diminished personal accomplishment* refers to a feeling of negative self-evaluation.

According to Leiter (1993) depersonalization is as a mechanism to cope with exhaustion where a worker tries to gain emotional distance from their recipients (e.g., treats a client as a number). Yet, many researchers have questioned the depersonalization as one of the component to burnout. E.g. Gaines and Jermier (1983) considered depersonalization as dispensable, Koeske and Koeske (1993) excluded this component from the burnout syndrome to reduce complexity. Still, Buunk and Schaufeli (1993) included this dimension after identifying depersonalization as relating directly to self-esteem. Leiter, (1993) further described that personal accomplishment includes the skill utilization, control, and coping with burnout. Many researchers had a belief that the lack of personal accomplishment is outside the scope of burnout or is not an important dimension of the burnout phenomenon (Gaines and Jermier, 1983; Jayaratne and Chess, 1984; Brookings et al., 1985). However, many other researchers (Buunk and Schaufeli, 1993; Leiter, 1993; Shirom, 1989) considered the MBI (Maslach Burnout Inventory) factor of emotional exhaustion to be the fundamental or core indicator of burnout and it seen to be the strongest factor of burnout (Wallace and Brinkerhoff, 1991).

Leiter and Maslach (1988) explained that there is a sequential development of different dimensions of burnout. Emotional exhaustion appears first as a consequence of the excessive demands at work. To survive in such a situation, the individual keeps himself away from his work and others as a defensive mechanism, and this leads to depersonalization or cynicism. As a sequel to this depersonalization, the capability of the employee to work efficiently decreases and when he realizes that his current undertakings do not match with his original expectations, it give rise to a sense of reduced personal accomplishment or inefficacy. In his model, developed later in 1991 on the basis of a study of mental health workers, Leiter (2001) described a framework of burnout that explored the effect of both the work context factors as well as coping styles on burnout. This model was advanced by Maslach, Schaufeli, and Leiter in 2001.

Cherniss' Transactional Process Model

Cherniss (1980) sees burnout as a process with three distinct stages involving job stress, strain, and defensive coping. He considered burnout to be a transactional process experienced as a self-perpetuating and self-reinforcing vicious cycle in which one reaction feeds into another till this established pattern is difficult to break.

Pines' and Aronson's Existential Model

In this model, burnout is defined and subjectively experienced as "a state of physical, emotional, and mental exhaustion caused by long-term involvement in situations that are emotionally demanding" (Pines and Aronson, 1988). They viewed it as intense damage to one's coping ability resulted due to the chronic existence of exceptionally tall expectations and situational stress. This Burnout Measure developed by them is a one-dimensional measure, which different from the MBI. Shirom (2003) criticized while developing this measure of burnout, Pines and Aronson (1988) have lost consideration to its operational definition.

Meier's Model of Burnout

Meier (1983) defined burnout as "a state in which individuals expect little reward and considerable punishment from work because of the lack of valued reinforcement, controllable outcomes, or personal competence". His framework is based on work of Bandura (1977), which viewed burnout from an interactions perspective, signifying that burnout is a consequence of not just the organizational factors; rather it emerges from interaction between the environment and the individual factors. Its four elements of burnout include: reinforcement expectations, outcome expectations, efficacy expectations, and contextual processing. But this model was unable to receive much support by later researches.

Smith's Cognitive-Affective Stress Model

Smith (1986) developed a four-stage model of burnout for athletes that considers the physiological, psychological, and behavioural dimensions of the process of stress and burnout, and the way these components influenced throughout by the individual's personality and their level of motivation. The four stages are: *Situational demands, Cognitive appraisal, Physiological responses, and Behavioural responses.* This model has specifically considered athletes for study. Thus, it may not be relevant for the employees working in corporates.

Moore's Attributional Model of Work Exhaustion

According to Moore (2000) situational factors like role overload, role ambiguity, role conflict, and lack of rewards have greater chances to work as the antecedents to work exhaustion rather than individual variables. he considered, two types of reactions could be experienced by the individual —either a straight result or outcome of the work exhaustion experience, i.e., attribution-independent attitudinal reactions or, the one resulting due to causal attribution that was earlier undertaken by the individual, i.e., attribution-dependent attitudinal reactions. Therefore, while one reaction is independent of the causal attribution (e.g., decreased job satisfaction), the other is totally contingent on the causal attribution (lower self-esteem at work). A group of several of components like attribution independent attitudinal reaction, attribution-dependent attitudinal reaction, characteristics of causal attribution and various situational and individual difference factors are expected to decide the behavior or an action taken by the individual as an effort to ease his work exhaustion. Those factors are depersonalization, voluntary turnover, efforts to alter the work situation, and efforts to change one. This process gives importance to the 'why' or the causes behind the occurrence of any 'unexpected, negative or important situation.' In the situation of work exhaustion, causal search can be considered as an individual's search for the reasons of his/her work exhaustion. The outcome of the causal search is the perception and understanding of the cause of the exhaustion.

Golembiewsky's Phase Model of Burnout

Golembiewsky's model has a base of Maslach's (1982) model of depersonalization, personal accomplishment, and emotional exhaustion. On the basis of the responses on Modified MBI (MMBI), the individual acquires definite scores on all the three dimensions, later on his score on every dimension is coded as high or low on the basis of available standards from a large population across the eight phases of burnout. As per the view of Leiter (1989) Golembiewsky's approach is deficient in empirical support; he had doubts about Golembiewsky's dichotomization procedure of the phases and criticizes the whole process of 'dichotomizing continuous scales.'

Sharma Burnout Scale (2007)

This scale is also based on MBI scale. Where author reveals that MBI that is developed in 1982 has mainly been based on people occupations (like nurses and teachers) and afterward extended to non-service occupations. After testing the same by Sharma (2007) in the context of Indian scenario on sample of executives, it discovered that there is a distinction in the dimension of diminished personal accomplishment which was not applicable in case the Indian respondents. It was seen that people suffering from burnout did not have low personal accomplishment; on the other hand, high achieving executives were mainly seen to get affected by burnout. Sharma's scale shows that emotional intelligence mediates and causes personal effectiveness which moderates the inception of burnout. Stress personality and personal inadequacy are found to be personality-related factors as predictors. She also found that role expectation conflict, role stagnation, self-role distance, role overload, role erosion, resource inadequacy, inter-role distance, and role ambiguity are role- related factors predicting of burnout among Indian executives.

Several demographic variables have been studied in relation to burnout, but the studies are relatively few and findings are not that consistent. (Schaufeli & Enxmann, 1998). Study by Tripathy (2002) shows that male managers are the higher burnouts in all three subscales, higher the qualification greater is the burnout, managers in the middle management cadre are the highest burnouts, and managers in the age range of 41 to 50 years and those having 21 to 30 years of total work experience show highest level of burnout.

2.5.3 Turnover Intent

Employee turnover is a serious problem for any organization. Many organizations invest in recruiting and retaining the best employees to reduce turnover. Organizations evaluate intention to turnover of present employees; this shows the extent of contribution of the employees. Researchers have defined turnover and turnover intention different research studies. Turnover intention is usually defined as seriously considering leaving one's current job (Guimaraes et al., 1992). It was conceived to be a conscious and deliberate wilfulness to leave the organization (Tett & Meyer, 1993).

Thought intention to leave does not measure actual turnover of employees, research has suggested that an individual's intentions to leave or stay is inclined to be a sufficient predictor of turnover behaviour (Fishbein and Ajzen, 1975; Locke, 1976; Mobley et al., 1978; Steel, Ovalle, 1984). Sager (1991) conducted longitudinal study of on salespeople, in which intention to quit was found to discriminate effectively between leavers and people with intention to stay. This study is an example of validity of studying intentions to quit an organization rather than actual quitting behaviour. Though turnover intention is not the same as voluntarily turnover, Igbaria and Greenhaus, (1992) have utilized intentions as indicative of actual quitting behaviour on the basis of the fact that intentions are the most direct determinants of actual quitting behaviour (Armitage and Connor, 2001; Kim and Hunter, 1983; Ajzen and Fishbein, 1980). While conducting a study of turnover on psychiatric nurses, Alexander et al. (1998) realized that intentions were vital predictors of turnover and that the greater part of variables in their model affected on turnover via intentions to quit. However, many researchers viz. Griffeth et al., (2000) and Hon and Griffeth (1995) have contended that intentions to quit do not elucidate a great amount of the variance in quitting behaviour. To support, Seston et al., (2009) found that relatively small proportion of employees have actually left the organization who showed intend to leave the job, suggesting that intentions may not be translated into action in this group of pharmacists.

If antecedents of turnover intent are examined, it will give better understanding to managers to design and reduce voluntary turnover. The Steers and Mowday (1981) described job attitudes other than satisfaction as antecedents to an employee's intentions to leave. It has also been seen that employee form an intention to quit when the perceived job alternatives in the market are considered be good (Hom et al., 1981; Sager et al., 1988).

Results by Arnold & Feldman (1982) indicate that turnover is significantly influenced by age, tenure in the organization, overall job satisfaction, organizational commitment, perceived job security, and intention to search for an alternative position. Further, it was discovered that different aspects of satisfaction e.g. pay, supervisory, co-worker, work were associated with intention to leave (Griffeth et al., 2000). Similarly, it has been over and over again observed that job dissatisfaction correlates with turnover intention (Cotton & Tuttle, 1986; Jaros, 1997; Lee & Mitchell, 1987; Sager et al., 1994). Hinshaw et al. (1987) contend that job stress indirectly affected turnover intentions through job satisfaction. The decrease in turnover and intention to leave is seen with the increase in the level of organizational fit (O'Reilly, Chatman, & Caldwell, 1991; Vandenberghe, 1999; Van Vianen, 2000). Similarly, organizational commitment has appeared to be a direct antecedent of employee intent to leave (Tett & Meyer, 1993). Some evidences also show that pay attitudes are related to commitment (Cohen & Gattiker, 1994) and quit intentions. The discrepancy model used by Jiang and Klein (2002) to study the difference between what employees want and how the organization satisfies those wants. The same has seen to affect the employee's intentions to leave the organization.

The body of theory on which turnover literature is based, is rooted primarily in the disciplines of psychology, sociology, and economics. The same can be seen by turnover models developed by various researchers. These models can be explained briefly as follows:

Mobley et al. (1979) model

This model depicts four key determinants of intentions to quit and consequently lead to turnover. Those factors are: job satisfaction – dissatisfaction, expected utility of alternative internal work roles, expected utility of external work roles, and non-work values and contingencies.

Moore's (2000) Turnover Model

Ellen Moore (2000) in this model studied work exhaustion as a possible mediating factor of turnover intention. His outcomes revealed that technology professionals with higher degrees of exhaustion depicted a higher intention to leave their job.

March and Simon Model

March and Simon's (1958) model of voluntary turnover is extensively used in the past literature today. It has been the most significant model in the research related to voluntary turnover, with modest done to change its original views. It is suggested in this model that ease of movement, known as perceived availability of job alternatives in today's literature, and desirability of movement known as job satisfaction are the two contributing factors of voluntary turnover. On the basis of the work by Meyer and Allen (1991) the traditional model voluntary turnover included organizational commitment. Their model considers three facets of organizational commitment.

Several research studies have been undertaken to establish the validity of the traditional model of turnover which consists job satisfaction, organizational commitment, and perceived availability of job alternatives. But, because of the relative novelty of Job Embeddedness, very less research has been done on testing its validity or relevance to different contexts and samples.

Lee and Mitchell's (1994) unfolding model of voluntary turnover

This model proposes two theories of how turnover occurs. They recommend the existence of a pull theory, which intends to focus on the external factors of an organization that are out of direct control such as an unsolicited job offer, spousal relocation, or other family obligations. On the other hand, a push theory is related to the organization forcing an employee to leave due to different organizational situations. For example, the organization may demand more time from the employees, compelling them to take a decision between family and work. This may lead to dissatisfaction among employees with organization and the same can result in their deteriorating commitment.

The new model of Job Embeddedness (Mitchell et al., 2001)

This model evaluates three seemingly distinctive constructs rather than the three in the traditional model. Job embeddedness consists of three diverse dimensions, which combines to structure one overall construct of job embeddedness. The first element in the job embeddedness construct is organizational links which is formed with the number of employees, teams, or work related projects the employee is directly linked with. This dimension studies the definite number of such links, as against a subjective attitudinal rating of the teams, employees, or work-related projects the employee is associated with. The second dimension is organizational fit which stand for how the employee perceives the compatibility with the organization, also well-known as person-organization fit. The third and last dimension of the job embeddedness is organizational sacrifices. It includes the costs of the employee leaving their current organization for another.

Rouse (2001) proposed that job dissatisfaction is the result of unmet need for achievement among employees. According to the models mentioned before, this job dissatisfaction will possibly lead to intention to leave.

The discrepancy model used by *Jiang and Klein (2002)* helps to scrutinize how the difference between what employees want and how the organization satisfies those wants affected the employee's intentions to leave the organization.

Ghapanchi & Aurum (2011) presented taxonomy of IT turnover antecedents comprising the five major categories: individual, organisational, job-related, psychological, and environmental factors.

The important finding from above turnover studies is that people who do not fit an environment well will tend to leave it (Mobley, 1982). Campion (1991) suggested that the turnover measures should be observed as lying on a continuum rather than on one of the two ends. Reduced employee turnover intent may be a sign of better employee retention. Shields and Ward (2000) find that nurses who report overall dissatisfaction with their jobs have a 65% higher probability of intending to quit than those reporting to be satisfied. Few research studies consider whether employees are at present thinking of quitting, and while other studies consider whether employees had thought of quitting during a specified time-period in the past (e.g., past 3 months) or if they had intended to leave within a designated time-period (Thatcher et al., 2002). The study by Kirschenbaum and Weisberg (2002) suggest that for the average worker, the probability of intent to quit is stronger when a change in job type is involved, regardless if it is in the same or different department or between organizations.

Apart from work and organizational related variables, individual variables influence turnover intent among employees of the organization. They are age, gender, tenure, education, and also marital status.

a steady negative relationship between age and turnover is observed in reviews of turnover literature. This shows that younger employees have exhibited a higher likelihood of leaving an organization (Mobley et al. 1979; Price 1977; Muchinski and Tuttle 1979; John Besich, 2005; Ahuja et al, 2007). An individual in the early career stage attempts to become established in a job that interests her or him, but if this job proves inappropriate, she or he opts to choose another job. Employees at this stage express greater intention to leave their organization and more willingness to relocate than those in other age groups (Orstein, Cron, & Slocum, 1989; Oenstein & Isabelta, 1990). Similarly, Griffeth et al. (1992) argued that occupational aspirations and concerns are formed by factors like age or work life experiences. Younger employees show more tendencies to move and have lesser psychological investment in the organization. In case of middle-aged employees the tendencies engage in behaviours is high which leads to stabilization. Finally, older employees are seen to usually involved in maintenance behaviours (Joseph et al., 2007). In contrast to this study, Baack, Luthans, and Rogers (1993) found that age positively correlated with protestant pastors' turnover intention.

It is observed that female workers have higher turnover than males (Marsh and Mannari, 1977; Lambert, 2006). In contrast to that, Joseph et al. (2007) contend that men generally report stronger intention to IT turnover. While Griffeth et al., 2000, have found gender to be unrelated to turnover intention.

It is found that tenure is negatively correlated with intention to leave (Baack, Luthans, and Rogers, 1993; Lambert, 2006). This means as tenure increased, the desire to leave decreased. Cascio (1997) found that tenure in the previous job, as part of a weighted application blank, was predictive of turnover. In contrast, few studies have found no relationship between tenure and turnover (Jurik & Winn, 1987; Ahuja et al., 2007) but many other studies have observed a relationship (e.g., Byrd, et al., 2000; Camp, 1994; Robinson, et al., 1997; Douglas Trimble 2006).

The significance of education as a variable is uncertain considering the large disparity in the quality of education (Mobley et al.). In addition to that, the lack of variation in education in studies such as Hellriegel and White (1983) prohibits sufficient evaluation of the relationship between an individual's education and their intention to leave. Still Lambert (2006) contends that in regards to education, those with a college degree were more likely to express turnover intent as compared to staff without a college degree.

2.6 Summary

An accurate and consistent theme throughout the literature is that organizations have the opportunity to reduce employee turnover and increase retention by utilizing appropriate selection processes, presenting applicants with realistic job previews, invoking certain organizational activities such as orientation programs, and analyzing data related to recruitment sources (Muchinsky & Tuttle, 1979; Rynes, 1991; Wanous, 1989). The vast majority of retention research shows retention and recruitment as two sides of the same coin (Fields, 2001). Fields pointed that retention and recruitment efforts are in fact intertwined. Buck and Watson (2002) also agreed to the interconnection between recruitment and retention. They proposed that by the use of suitable recruitment processes, and sharing realistic job previews to the potential new employees, and implementing effective orientation programs in fact lowered employee turnover. Carpitella (2002) further supported to the fact by stating that poor supervision, little direction, and unfulfilled job expectations during the intial stages of employment, are vital reasons of employee turnover. As oppose to this orientation practices such as meaningful supervision, direction, and alignment of job expectation to performance need is seen to be convincing indicators of employee retention.

2.7 Research Gap

All prior studies in the stream of recruitment research used college students as subjects and the school/ college campuses as a field of recruitment (Rynes & Miller, 1983; Harris & Fink, 1987; Taylor & Bergmann, 1987; Powell, 1991). Harris (1989) also noted that all of the research he reviewed involved college student reactions to campus interviews and questioned generalizability of other jobs. Thus, it becomes essential to consider applicants from other than college students, and campus recruitments to better understand recruitment and retention aspects.

Apart from for the literature on realistic job previews (Premack & Wanous, 1985; Wanous, 1973), prior empirical research has offered little information about how applicants react to diverse recruitment activities or about the stubbornness of their responses over time. Therefore, there is requirement for research that to enlarge recruitment outcomes on various dimensions.

Applicants with greater work experience have greater awareness of work environment and so they may be influenced less by recruiting practices, and focus more on job attributes (Powell, 1984). These studies have considered immediate effects (i.e. immediately after interview, one week after the recruitment process, etc.) of recruitment practices on applicant reactions i.e. their job choice decision, attributes of recruiter, interview experience, etc (Powell, 1984; Harris & Fink, 1987). Recruitment process can have long term effect on the candidates and the same is needed to be tested. In contrast to that Harris (1989) stated that recruiting practices affect applicant reactions only for a specified duration because of the applicant's peripheral processing of information at the time of interview. Studies that assessed applicant reactions immediately after the interview, such as Harris & Fink (1987) would be most likely to show an effect of recruiting practices. Barber (1998) suggested that previous research has failed to paint a compelling picture regarding relationships between recruitment source and post-hire outcomes. Thus, further research needs to be conducted to understand long term effects of recruitment activities on their retention.

It is observed that recruitment researchers tend to ignore that companies implement recruitment strategies differently and also the possibility that their effectiveness may differ with the organizational context in which they are implemented (Rynes & Barber, 1990; Taylor & Collins, 2000). Therefore, next level of research should consider organizational context to understand recruitment and retention in the same.

Most of the research on recruitment and retention has studied employees in the United States or other western countries. Less information is available on these aspects among employees in countries that constitute a significantly different institutional and cultural context. In particular, little is known about the relationship between recruitment and retention among employees in India.

Hausknecht et al. (2004) recommend in their study that to enhance generalizability of applicant reaction research, studies should explore reactions by working professional, older workers, and applicants to private industry. They also contend that process of recruitment might differ for individuals who are applying for senior-level and executive positions as compared to that of entry level or public sector personnel. Additionally, older workers may hold different view towards recruitment procedure from their younger counterparts. Therefore, consideration of individual variables should be made for better understanding of recruitment and employee retention.

The majority of the previous research has paid attention to the aspect as to why employees leave once they are in an organization. Very less research is available which has investigated whether employers can reduce turnover at selection (Barrick & Zimmerman, 2005). Thus, purpose of this study is to systematically explore whether applicants with high turnover propensities can be identified and avoided prior to organizational entry.

Thus, the current work is based on the assumption that it is still interesting to study post-hire outcomes (retention) of recruitment sources.

2.8 Hypotheses

Robertson et al. (1991) has shown that reaction to selection procedures can be related to organizational commitment and intentions to leave. Research on realistic recruiting practices has suggested that if individuals make job choices with artificially high expectations of what they will experience at work, lower satisfaction and higher turnover are more likely than with realistic expectations (Wanous, 1976, 1977).

Considering the review of literature by various researchers mentioned in previous section and views of Robertson et al. (1991), Wanous (1976, 1977) hypotheses are developed. They are stated as follows:

Major Hypothesis

H_0: There is no significant relationship between recruitment strategies and categories of employee retention.

H_1: There is significant relationship between recruitment strategies and categories of employee retention.

Minor Hypotheses

Major hypothesis is stated with the following minor hypotheses.

Literature points out inconsistencies between findings of survey and empirical research on source effectiveness and suggests the need for further research focusing on the causes of differential effectiveness. Taylor (1983) strongly supports the utility of identifying and studying the effects of individual characteristics in future studies of recruitment source effectiveness.

1. H_0: There is no significant relationship between recruitment sources and committed employees retained in the organization.

   H_1: There is significant relationship between recruitment sources and committed employees retained in the organization.

2. H_0: There is no significant relationship between recruitment sources and burnout employees in the organization.

   H_1: There is significant relationship between recruitment sources and burnout employees in the organization.

3. H_0: There is no significant relationship between recruitment sources and turnover intention of employees.

   H_1: There is significant relationship between recruitment sources and turnover intention of employees.

Individuals will try to justify job choices (O'Reilly & Caldwell, 1981). Any post hoc study of job applicants' information use must take into account individuals' reactions to jobs. Without accounting for these individual reactions, we cannot separate prospective use of information from retrospective reports of use of information. Thus, the objective of this research is to find out the relationship between information shared with the applicants and type of employees retained in the organization.

4. H_0: There is no significant relationship between information shared and committed employees in the organization.

   H_1: There is significant relationship between information shared and committed employees in the organization.

5. H_0: There is no significant relationship between information shared and burnout employees in the organization.

   H_1: There is significant relationship between information shared and burnout employees in the organization.

A review of 11 studies (Reilly, Brown, Blood, & Malatesta, 1981) reported that turnover was significantly lower than expected across studies for individuals who had received realistic job preview information. A study by Caldwell and O'Reilly (1985) show that individuals who report that they have received accurate information about jobs are less likely to leave their organizations than are those who have received inaccurate information. Thus, hypothesis is framed as:

6. H_0: There is no significant relationship between information shared and turnover intention of employees.

   H_1: There is significant relationship between information shared and turnover intention of employees.

Taylor and Bergmann (1987) found that recruitment activities had no effect on applicant reactions across different stages in the recruitment process. Further research is needed to test this more carefully. In their recommendations, Harris & Fink (1987) suggested to determine whether the impact of recruiter is merely temporary or has permanent effect on applicant perception.

7. H_0: There is no significant relationship between recruiter & recruitment process and committed employees in the organization.

    H_1: There is significant relationship between recruiter & recruitment process and committed employees in the organization.

8. H_0: There is no significant relationship between recruiter & recruitment process and burnout employees in the organization.

    H_1: There is significant relationship between recruiter & recruitment process and burnout employees in the organization.

9. H_0: There is no significant relationship between recruiter & recruitment process and turnover intention of employees.

    H_1: There is significant relationship between recruiter & recruitment process and turnover intention of employees.

None of the research studies mentioned in the literature review section explain applicants' reaction to interview process and also its long term relationship with employee behaviour (Taylor & Bergmann, 1987) in terms of retention.

10. H_0: There is no significant relationship between interview structure and committed employees in the organization.

    H_1: There is significant relationship between interview structure and committed employees in the organization.

11. H_0: There is no significant relationship between interview structure and burnout employees in the organization.

H_1: There is significant relationship between interview structure and burnout employees in the organization.

12. H_0: There is no significant relationship between interview structure and turnover intention of employees.

    H_1: There is significant relationship between interview structure and turnover intention of employees.

Both theoretical and empirical works have suggested that variations in attraction practices can have important effects on long-term (i.e., post-acceptance) outcomes as well. For example, organization applicant interactions may influence applicants' subsequent decisions to stay committed or leave the organization. Decisions to enhance attraction inducements (e.g., housing assistance, higher starting salaries) have been shown to lead to reduced turnover (Hamlet, 1989; Lakhani, 1988).

13. H_0: There is no significant relationship between applicant attractors and committed employees in the organization.

    H_1: There is significant relationship between applicant attractors and committed employees in the organization.

14. H_0: There is no significant relationship between applicant attractors and burnout employees in the organization.

    H_1: There is significant relationship between applicant attractors and burnout employees in the organization.

15. H_0: There is no significant relationship between applicant attractors and turnover intention of employees.

    H_1: There is significant relationship between applicant attractors and turnover intention of employees.

2.9 Concept Map

Hypotheses mentioned in the previous section are diagrammatically represented with the help of following concept map:

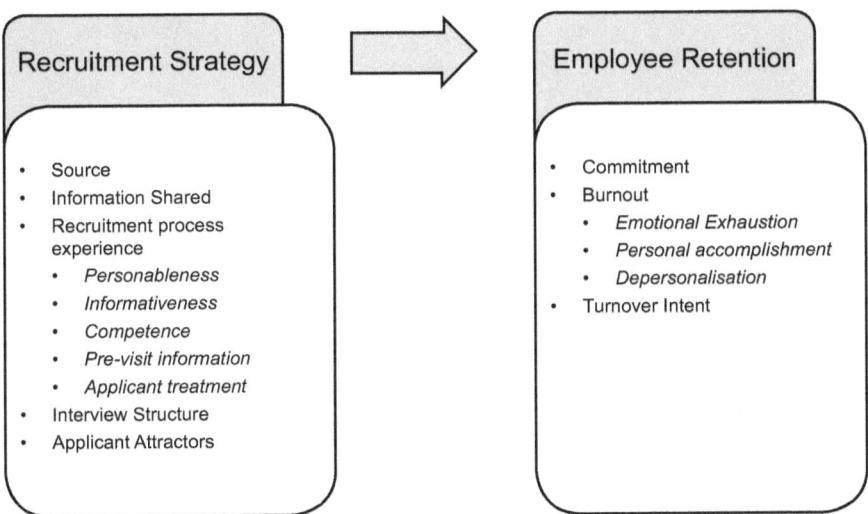

Figure 2.5 – Concept Map

In order to collect data and analyze the same, appropriate methodology is designed and presented in the next chapter. The next chapter also includes sampling and method of data collection.

CHAPTER III

RESEARCH METHODOLOGY

3.1 Chapter Overview

This chapter outlines methods incorporated to investigate the relationship between recruitment strategy and employee retention. The type of study is explained. The research sampling is described with sample plan and samples used. The operational definition of independent and dependent variables is explained. It also states tools of measurement of variables studied. This chapter concludes with procedure used in data collection for the study.

3.2 Type of Study

It is an exploratory study undertaken to ascertain and describe the characteristics of recruitment strategy and employee retention variables. Hypotheses are developed to assess the nature of relationship or differences among variables. Specifically, the present study is aimed at capturing the recruitment strategy in a holistic way; and finds its relationship with the type of employees retained in the organization. The first aim is descriptive in nature. The second aim is pursued through series of hypotheses.

This study is developed on the basis of literature review of research conducted considering different variables one at a time. Aim of this research is to consider together all those variables of recruitment strategy, considered by the earlier researchers, to conduct its holistic study and find its overall relationship with retention i.e. dependent variable. Thus, first step is to find correlation of independent and dependent variables. Further, multiple regression analysis is conducted to find the strength of relationship between those variables.

The present study is designed on the basis of the theoretical and methodological considerations. As far as the latter is concerned, there have been certain practical, externally imposed constraints that did not permit the researcher to follow the methodological considerations, that is, to employ a longitudinal design. This cross-sectional study was designed to examine the relationship of recruitment strategy with employee retention. This study is not of predictive nature but it attempts to find the relationship between recruitment strategy and employee retention.

This chapter includes a description of the population under study, data collection methods, survey instrument development, and the statistical techniques that are used to analyze the data.

3.3 Sampling

The research data on applicant impressions is gathered exclusively from applicants. Due to the sensitive nature of the questions, all respondents were guaranteed anonymity, and no specific data that might identify the respondent was solicited. For generalization purpose not more than 70 responses were collected from single organization.

A certain amount of tenure is necessary in order to assess retention of employees. So those employees who have completed one year in the organization were considered for the study. Also, as employees have to give their opinion about recruitment experience only those employees who have been employed for not more than 5 years were considered. The reason being such employees might not be able to clearly recollect their recruitment experience after five years of tenure in the organization.

There are 22 private sector banks, 33 co-operative banks, and 40 foreign banks operating in India. Similarly, there are 24 life insurance companies and 28 general insurance companies operating in India. Out of these organizations 10 private sector banks, 6 co-operative banks, 9 foreign banks, 10 life insurance companies, and 11 general insurance companies are randomly identified for the study. Three organizations from each category are randomly identified for interviews with HR heads and recruitment heads.

To collect data from bank and insurance professionals, researcher approached various banks and insurance companies with request to them to give details of the employees having zero to 5 years of tenure in their current organization, working at different managerial levels, across geographical locations in India. Researcher had approached respondents personally through face to face meetings, telephone, and e-mails.

The sample for the study consists of 591 employees at three levels in organizations i.e. entry level managers, middle level managers and top managers working in 46 private, foreign and co-operative banks as well as private and foreign insurance, both life and general insurance companies, operating in India. 25% of the respondents are working in co-operative banks, 26% in private banks, 14% in foreign banks, 14% in general insurance companies, and 20% in life insurance companies operating in India.

Out of total 591 respondents, 67% are males. 12% of them are below 25 years of age, 73% are of age between 25 to 35 years, 12% are of age between 35 to 45 years, 2% between 45 to 55 years, and 1% have age above 55 years. 47% of respondents have bachelor degree, 34% master degree, and 17% professional degree. Out of 591 respondents 47% have tenure of 1 year to 3 years in current organization. 17% have experience of 3 years to 5 years in current organization, while 15% of them have more than 5 years of tenure in current organization. The total experience in banking and insurance sector is also considered in this study. Amongst all respondents 25% have experience of 1 year to 3 years in the industry, 27% have 3 years to 5 years of total experience, and 40% of respondents have more than 5 years of experience in the industry.

3.4 Variables and Operational Definitions

Due to the nature of the recruitment process, different activities are measured. The specific recruitment activities measured in the study were selected on the basis of findings and suggestions from three sources: previous research, applicants (at pilot study), and company HR heads as well as recruitment heads. Items were identified to tap the relevant activity and were revised based on the comments from applicants and company recruiters. The operational definition of variables is explained below:

3.4.1 Recruitment strategy – Independent Variables

Recruitment strategy is defined as a collection of decisions regarding source of recruitment, information shared with the applicant, recruiter and recruitment process followed, interviewer and interview structure, and applicant attractor factors used by the organization.

Source of Recruitment

The components of source of recruitment is considered from Klaus Moser (2005)'s study. It contains mainly two sources of recruitment i.e. Internal and External. Internal source includes recruiting by referrals, rehires, and in-house notices. While external sources include recruitment through job advertisements, employment agencies, search firms, school/ college campus, and walk-ins. Single items are used for assessing this information.

Information Shared

The study considers attributes of information shared on job facets by Caldwell and O'Reilly III (1985). Those attributes are information on salary and benefits, career paths, content of work, working conditions, co-workers, level of responsibility, and training and development. These attributes were measured on a dimension of realisticity, specificity, and whether shared on time or not, as suggested by Philips (1998), and Frank Mianzo (2005) in their study.

Recruitment Process Experience

Various researchers have suggested that two recruiter characteristics account for the most variance in overall applicant reactions: how personable the recruiter is (caring, empathetic, or concerned), and how informed or informative the recruiter is (about the applicant, job, and company) (Harris & Fink, 1987; Herriot & Rothwell, 1981; Powell, 1991; Turban & Dougherty, 1992).

In today's world of information technology, organizations are making use of communication technology like telephone, internet, and video-conferencing for smooth functioning of recruitment activities. This has led to lack of face to face contact of applicants with organization representative, who can act as a recruiter. The only face to face conversation applicant has is with the interviewers. Thus, recruiter characteristics like personableness, and informativeness are least experienced by the applicants during recruitment process. But applicants can experience the personableness and informativeness of the organization as a recruiter.

The attributes of recruitment process experience considered are personableness, informativeness, competence of organization as a recruiter, previsit information shared, and applicant treatment during recruitment. These attributes are measured on a five point Likert's scale. Cronbach Alpha is 0.86

Interview Structure

The components of interview structure are explained by various researchers like Yates (1988), Campion, Plamer & Campion (1998), Hyde (1997), Downs (1969), Engler-Parish & Miller (1989), Fletcher (1989), Rynes, Bretz & Gerhart (1991), Taylor & Sniezek (1984). After reviewing attributes, those attributes considered for the study are informedness of interviewer, questions by applicants, content of discussion, time spent during interview. These components of interview structure are measured on a five point Likert's scale. Cronbach Alpha is 0.88

Applicant Attractors

The study has adapted attributes developed by Steven Ralston & Robert Brady (1994). Their tool is based on prior research (cf. Bergman & Taylor, 1984; Harris & Fink, 1987; Powell, 1984, 1991; Rynes & Miller, 1983). The attributes of applicant attractor considered for the study are use of benefits, job security, training, career advancement opportunities, salary, reputation, growth, management philosophy, and geographic location options given by organization during recruitment process. These attributes are measured on 5 point Likert's scale. Cronbach Alpha is 0.88.

3.4.2 Employee Retention – Dependent Variables

Research by Barbara Kreisman (2002) demonstrates that the working population or retained employees can be categorized as: people who are engaged (loyal and productive), those who are not engaged (just putting in time), and those who are actively disengaged (unhappy and spreading their discontent). Specifically, employee retention is categorised into three types of employees staying with the organization namely, committed, burnouts, and employees with turnover intent. The measure can be explained as follows:

Commitment

Employee commitment is measured by the 15-item Organizational Commitment Questionnaire (OCQ) (Porter et al., 1974), which has demonstrated good psychometric properties and has been used with a wide range of job categories (Mowday, Steers, and Porter, 1979). The study makes use of 7 point Litert's scale for its measurement. Cronbach Alpha is 0.83.

Burnout

As per a study by Schaufeli and Dierendonck (1993) the MBI – Maslach Burnout Index (Maslach and Jackson, 1981) can be employed as a reliable and valid multi-dimensional indicator of burnout in professionals who work with people. MBI assess three components of burnout: emotional exhaustion, depersonalization, and low personal accomplishment. The same is adapted here for the study on 7 point Likert's scale. Cronbach Alpha is 0.89 of Emotional exhaustion, 0.82 of Personal Accomplishment, and of Depersonalization it is 0.74

Turnover Intent

Turnover intention is operationalized as the likelihood that a person will seek employment elsewhere rather than remaining in his/her present job (John Besich, 2005). For this study purpose the five point Likert's measurement scale developed by Mak and Sockel (2001) is adapted. Cronbach Alpha is 0.82

3.5 Control Variables

The control variables of the study are stated as follows:
- Banking and insurance sector in India
- Tenure of respondents

3.6 Tools of Measurement

The studies that are considered for developing scale are summarized in the following table:

Table 3.1: Measures

Variable	Studies considered	Data Scale	Cronbach Alpha
Recruitment Strategy			
Source of Recruitment	Klaus Moser (2005), Fisher et al. (2005)	Nominal Data	–
Information shared	Caldwell & O'Reilly III (1985) and Philips (1998)	Nominal Data	–
Recruitment process experience	Harris & Fink (1987) and Taylor & Bergman (1987)	Interval Data	0.857
Interview structure	Jablin & McComb (1984) and Harris & Fink (1987)	Interval Data	0.883
Applicant Attractors	Ralston & Brady (1994)	Interval Data	0.879
Employee Retention			
Commitment	Porter, Steers, & Mowday (1974)	Interval Data	0.827
Burnout	Maslach et al., (1981)		
	Emotional Exhaustion	Interval Data	0.896
	Personal Accomplishment	Interval Data	0.824
	Depersonalization	Interval Data	0.743
Turnover Intent	Mak and Sockel (2001)	Interval Data	0.821

3.7 Data Collection

A survey questionnaire was developed to collect the data on various dimensions. The same was administered among the bank and insurance employees. A letter of invitation to share the data was given by the supervisor to each of the participating organizations. Questionnaire with a copy of this invitation letter and an appeal to respondents was given in the beginning of the survey questionnaire. The participating organizations were assured confidentiality of the data collected from their employees. Employees were also assured that their responses will be kept confidential and only consolidated data of all responses will be shared with concerned authorities in the organization.

The interference of the researcher was minimal to the extent of interviewing HR and recruitment heads and administering questionnaire personally amongst the selected employees of the banks and insurance companies.

The data so collected was analyzed and is presented in the next chapter. It also includes discussion of the results.

CHAPTER IV

DATA ANALYSIS, HYPOTHESIS TESTING AND DISCUSSION

4.1 Chapter Overview

The purpose of this study is to gain enhanced understanding of the components of recruitment strategy that influence employee retention in terms of commitment, burnout and, turnover intent. Data is analysed using Statistical Analysis System (SAS). This chapter presents data analysis in four subsections. First section contains details of cronbach's alpha; second, descriptive statistics; third correlation analysis and; fourth, regression analysis.

4.2 Cronbach Alpha

The analysis of questionnaire commenced by testing is construct reliability. Table 4.1 presents the results of the internal consistency of each scale measured by Cronbach alpha coefficients. The reliability coefficients of all the measurement scales (except source of recruitment and information shared) show strong reliability i.e. above .70. As source of recruitment and information shared reports categorical data, Cronbach's alpha cannot be calculated for them.

Table 4.1 - Cronbach Alpha

Variable	Cronbach Alpha	Number of Item
Recruitment Strategy		
Source of Recruitment	Parametric data	1
Information shared	Parametric data	7
Recruitment process experience	0.857	18
Interview structure	0.883	7
Applicant Attractors	0.879	9
Employee Retention		
Commitment	0.827	15
Burnout		
Emotional Exhaustion	0.896	9
Personal Accomplishment	0.824	8
Depersonalization	0.743	5
Turnover Intent	0.821	5

Descriptive Statistics

This section depicts descriptive statistics of dependent and independent variables. Table 4.2 shows that respondents found the recruitment process to be highly personable (3.64), informative (3.64), and competent (3.75). Good amount of pre-visit information was shared (3.18) with them during recruitment process. While the treatment (2.76) given to them during recruitment was moderately satisfying. Interviews were highly (4.05) structured according to respondents. Higher level of attraction (3.90) is seen among the applicants towards organization. The respondents from banking and insurance sector are highly committed (4.99) to their organization. Similarly, their level of emotional exhaustion (1.60), personal accomplishment (1.88), and depersonalization (1.50) is seen to be low. However, standard deviations in all three are also very high as compared to the respective areas. In spite of high level of commitment and low level of burnout (emotional exhaustion, personal accomplishment, and depersonalization) their intention to leave (2.78) is moderately high.

Table 4.2 – Descriptive Statistics

Variable	Mean	Std Dev	Minimum	Maximum
Recruitment Process Experience				
Personable	3.6370	0.6233	1.0000	5.0000
Informativeness	3.6432	0.8390	1.0000	5.0000
Competence	3.7538	0.5691	1.7500	5.0000
PrevisitInfo	3.1813	0.8462	1.1111	5.0000
Applicant Treatment	2.7630	0.5039	0.6667	4.5000
Interviewer Structure	4.0487	0.5763	1.0000	5.0000
Applicant Attractors	3.8970	0.6324	1.0000	5.0000
Commitment	4.9924	0.9202	1.5333	7.0000
Burnout				
Emotional Exhaustion	1.6031	1.3465	0.0000	6.0000
Personal Accomplishment	1.8780	1.2299	0.0000	6.0000
Depersonalization	1.5008	1.3123	0.0000	6.0000
Turnover Intent	2.7722	0.9745	1.0000	5.0000

N = 591

Table 4.3 below shows that mean value of Commitment (5.07) among female is higher than mean value of commitment (4.95) among male respondents. It is seen that level of burnout (i.e emotional exhaustion, personal accomplishment, and depersonalization) is low among both male and female respondents. Also standard deviations in each of these, as compared to the respective means, are high. Mean value of turnover intent is 2.82 among male respondents while the same is 2.69 among female respondents.

Table 4.3 - Summary Statistics by Gender

Gender	N	Variable	Mean	SD
Male	394	Commitment	4.95	0.93
		Emotional	1.68	1.36
		Personal Accomplishment	1.86	1.25
		Depersonalization	1.68	1.33
		Turnover Intent	2.82	0.98
Female	197	Commitment	5.07	0.90
		Emotional Exhaustion	1.45	1.31
		Personal Accomplishment	1.91	1.19
		Depersonalization	1.14	1.19
		Turnover Intent	2.69	0.97

(P values: Loyalty (0.1571), Emotional Exhaustion (0.0566), Personal Accomplishment (0.6289), Depersonalization (<0.0001), Turnover Intent (0.1172))

Table 4.4 depicts mean values and standard deviation of commitment, burnout and turnover intent among various age groups. Respondents below 25 years of age show the highest mean value 5.12 of commitment compared to other age groups. Mean value of emotional exhaustion and depersonalization is low among all the age groups. While mean value of personal accomplishment is the highest among age group of 55-65 years (3.63) followed by age group of 45-55 years (3.11). Emotional exhaustion, personal accomplishment, and depersonalization have high standard deviation as compared to the respective mean values. Respondents of age group 35-45 years show the highest level of turnover intent (2.83) followed by age group 25-35 years (2.81) and age group below 25 years (2.70).

Table 4.4 - Summary Statistics by Age

Age	N	Variable	Mean	SD
Below 25 yrs	73	Commitment	5.12	0.87
		Emotional Exhaustion	1.45	1.34
		Personal Accomplishment	1.99	1.25
		Depersonalization	1.47	1.24
		Turnover Intent	2.70	0.90
25–35 yrs	432	Commitment	4.95	0.92
		Emotional Exhaustion	1.68	1.35
		Personal Accomplishment	1.87	1.21
		Depersonalization	1.54	1.33
		Turnover Intent	2.81	0.97
35–45 yrs	73	Commitment	5.09	0.95
		Emotional Exhaustion	1.45	1.38
		Personal Accomplishment	1.55	1.04
		Depersonalization	1.37	1.31
		Turnover Intent	2.83	1.03
45–55 yrs	10	Commitment	4.99	0.98
		Emotional Exhaustion	0.81	0.65
		Personal Accomplishment	3.11	1.49
		Depersonalization	1.32	1.16
		Turnover Intent	1.94	0.81
55–65 yrs	2	Commitment	4.97	1.18
		Emotional Exhaustion	0.94	0.71
		Personal Accomplishment	3.63	2.83
		Depersonalization	0.90	0.99
		Turnover Intent	1.70	0.71

(P values: Loyalty (0.5510), Emotional Exhaustion (0.1274), Personal Accomplishment (0.0005), Depersonalization (0.7993), Turnover Intent (0.0259))

Table 4.5 shows level of commitment, burnout, and turnover intent amongst respondents with different levels of qualification. Mean value of commitment (5.71) is the highest amongst the respondents who have secured qualification other than bachelor degree, master, professional, or doctoral degree followed by respondents who have secured bachelors degree (5.07).

Table 4.5 - Summary statistics by Education Level

Educational Level	N	Variable	Mean	SD
Bachelor Degree	280	Commitment	5.07	0.89
		Emotional Exhaustion	1.53	1.34
		Personal Accomplishment	1.85	1.20
		Depersonalization	1.58	1.32
		Turnover Intent	2.74	0.96
Master Degree	204	Commitment	4.87	0.91
		Emotional Exhaustion	1.63	1.29
		Personal Accomplishment	1.92	1.17
		Depersonalization	1.44	1.32
		Turnover Intent	2.92	0.97
Professional Degree	99	Commitment	5.02	1.02
		Emotional Exhaustion	1.78	1.49
		Personal Accomplishment	1.82	1.34
		Depersonalization	1.42	1.30
		Turnover Intent	2.63	0.99
Doctoral Degree	4	Commitment	4.35	0.52
		Emotional Exhaustion	1.64	0.39
		Personal Accomplishment	4.09	1.82
		Depersonalization	1.65	0.57
		Turnover Intent	1.90	0.68
Other	4	Commitment	5.71	0.47
		Emotional Exhaustion	0.89	1.10
		Personal Accomplishment	0.97	0.66
		Depersonalization	0.65	1.05
		Turnover Intent	2.60	1.07

(P values: Loyalty (0.0362), Emotional Exhaustion (0.4615), Personal Accomplishment (0.0032), Depersonalization (0.4770), Turnover Intent (0.0317))

Burnout (i.e emotional exhaustion, personal accomplishment, and depersonalization) in the above table is seen to be low among all categories of respondents except personal accomplishment among doctoral degree holders (4.09). However, standard deviation of emotional exhaustion, personal accomplishment, and depersonalization is high as compared to the respective means, except those having doctoral degree. Mean value of turnover intent is the highest among people with master's degree (2.92) and lowest among respondents with doctoral degree (1.90).

Table 4.6 shows mean values and standard deviation of commitment, burnout, and turnover intent of respondents with certain tenure in their current organization. Respondents with less than 12 months (5.20) of experience show the highest mean value of commitment.

Table 4.6 - Summary Statistics by Current Organization Experience

Current Organization Experience	N	Variable	Mean	SD
Less than 12 months	120	Commitment	5.20	0.95
		Emotional Exhaustion	1.30	1.22
		Personal Accomplishment	1.70	1.14
		Depersonalization	1.21	1.25
		Turnover Intent	2.48	0.87
1–3 yrs	279	Commitment	4.95	0.93
		Emotional Exhaustion	1.70	1.46
		Personal Accomplishment	1.97	1.28
		Depersonalization	1.55	1.35
		Turnover Intent	2.81	1.01
3–5 yrs	103	Commitment	4.85	0.89
		Emotional Exhaustion	1.72	1.22
		Personal Accomplishment	1.98	1.33
		Depersonalization	1.56	1.22
		Turnover Intent	2.97	0.92
More than 5 yrs	4	Commitment	5.01	0.86
		Emotional Exhaustion	1.58	1.25
		Personal Accomplishment	1.71	1.07
		Depersonalization	1.67	1.35
		Turnover Intent	2.85	0.97

(P values: Loyalty (0.0234), Emotional Exhaustion (0.0400), Personal Accomplishment (0.0986), Depersonalization (0.0496), Turnover Intent (0.0013))

Mean values of burnout (emotional exhaustion, personal accomplishment, and depersonalization) are low among all categories of respondents with high standard deviation as compared to the respective means. Mean value of turnover intent is highest (2.97) amongst the respondents with 3-5 years of experience in current organization.

Table 4.7 depicts statistics by total experience of respondents in banking and insurance sector. It is seen that respondents with less than 12 months of total experience in the industry show the highest level of mean commitment (5.50) compared to those who have more than 1 year of experience in the industry. Mean values of burnout (emotional exhaustion, personal accomplishment, and depersonalization) are low among all categories of respondents with high standard deviation as compared to respective means. Mean value of turnover intent is the highest among those respondents who have total experience of 3 to 5 years (2.85) and above.

Table 4.7 - Summary Statistics by Total Experience

Total Experience	N	Variable	Mean	SD
Less than 12 months	51	Commitment	5.50	1.91
		Emotional Exhaustion	1.19	1.20
		Personal Accomplishment	1.71	1.00
		Depersonalization	1.05	1.12
		Turnover Intent	2.39	0.77
1–3 yrs	145	Commitment	5.02	0.95
		Emotional Exhaustion	1.49	1.37
		Personal Accomplishment	1.96	1.23
		Depersonalization	1.46	1.26
		Turnover Intent	2.71	1.03
3–5 yrs	159	Commitment	4.86	0.92
		Emotional Exhaustion	1.80	1.41
		Personal Accomplishment	2.06	1.33
		Depersonalization	1.66	1.34
		Turnover Intent	2.85	0.96
More than 5 yrs	236	Commitment	4.96	0.87
		Emotional Exhaustion	1.63	1.30
		Personal Accomplishment	1.74	1.19
		Depersonalization	1.51	1.35
		Turnover Intent	2.85	0.97

(P values: Loyalty (0.0002), Emotional Exhaustion (0.0238), Personal Accomplishment (0.0479), Depersonalization (0.0399), Turnover Intent (0.0111))

Table 4.8 has summarized level of commitment, burnout, and turnover intent among respondents from different management levels in organizations studied. Mean value of commitment is the highest amongst the respondents from top management level (5.06) in the organizations while the same is the lowest amongst the respondents from junior management level (4.99) in the organizations studied though the difference between them is not very high. Mean values of Burnout (i.e. emotional exhaustion, personal accomplishment, and depersonalization) are low among all categories of respondents with high standard deviation as compared to the respective means. While mean value of turnover intent is the highest among the middle management level (2.80) of respondents and the same is the lowest among top management level (2.29) of respondents.

Table 4.8 - Summary Statistics by Management level

Mgmt. Level	N	Variable	Mean	SD
Junior Mgt Level	297	Commitment	4.99	0.96
		Emotional Exhaustion	1.58	1.43
		Personal Accomplishment	1.83	1.20
		Depersonalization	1.53	1.30
		Turnover Intent	2.78	0.98
Middle Mgt Level	276	Commitment	5.00	0.88
		Emotional Exhaustion	1.65	1.27
		Personal Accomplishment	1.90	1.22
		Depersonalization	1.47	1.33
		Turnover Intent	2.80	0.97
Top Mgt Level	17	Commitment	5.06	0.89
		Emotional Exhaustion	1.31	1.11
		Personal Accomplishment	2.44	1.81
		Depersonalization	1.54	1.29
		Turnover Intent	2.29	1.02

(P values: Loyalty (0.9494), Emotional Exhaustion (0.5615), Personal Accomplishment (0.1278), Depersonalization (0.8385), Turnover Intent (0.1135))

Table 4.9 below gives details on mean values of commitment, burnout and turnover intent among respondents from various types of organizations like co-operative banks, private banks, and foreign banks operating in India, private Indian insurance companies, and foreign insurance companies operating in India. The mean value of commitment is the highest for respondents from co-operative banks (5.29), while the same is the lowest for respondents from private banks (4.65).

Table 4.9 - Summary Statistics by Type of Organization

Type of Organization	N	Variable	Mean	SD
Co-operative Banks	147	Commitment	5.29	0.76
		Emotional Exhaustion	1.03	1.07
		Personal Accomplishment	1.66	1.11
		Depersonalization	1.31	1.17
		Turnover Intent	2.44	0.92
Private Banks	155	Commitment	4.65	1.04
		Emotional Exhaustion	2.12	1.52
		Personal Accomplishment	2.06	1.30
		Depersonalization	1.73	1.38
		Turnover Intent	3.03	1.02
Foreign Banks	84	Commitment	4.78	0.87
		Emotional Exhaustion	1.74	1.16
		Personal Accomplishment	1.97	1.21
		Depersonalization	1.53	1.26
		Turnover Intent	2.96	0.84
Private Insurance Companies	84	Commitment	5.25	0.83
		Emotional Exhaustion	1.43	1.33
		Personal Accomplishment	1.93	1.43
		Depersonalization	1.35	1.45
		Turnover Intent	2.56	0.91
Foreign Insurance Companies	118	Commitment	5.02	0.86
		Emotional Exhaustion	1.68	1.27
		Personal Accomplishment	1.82	1.13
		Depersonalization	1.53	1.30
		Turnover Intent	2.88	0.98

(P values: Loyalty (<0.0001), Emotional Exhaustion (<0.0001), Personal Accomplishment (0.0680), Depersonalization (0.0626), Turnover Intent (<0.0001))

Mean value of emotional exhaustion (2.12) and personal accomplishment (2.06) are the highest among respondents from private sector banks. However, standard deviations of emotional exhaustion, personal accomplishment, and depersonalization are high as compared to the respective means. Similarly, mean value of turnover intent is the highest (3.03) among private banks respondents and the same is the (2.44) least among co-operative banks respondents.

4.4 Correlation Analysis:

Recruitment Strategy and Employee Retention

The scale correlations are calculated between the independent variables and dependent variable. In table 4.10 the correlation matrix presents the relationship between four measures of recruitment strategies namely Information shared, Recruitment process experience, interview structure, and applicant attractors and, the various employee retention variables like commitment, burnout, and turnover intent. All the coefficients of correlation are statistically significant at 5% level of significance.

Table 4.10 – Correlation Analysis

Pearson Correlation Coeffiecients Prob > |r| uner H0' Rho = 0					
	Commitment	Burnout			Turn Int
		Emotional Exhaustion	Personal Accompl	Depersnln	
Information Shared	0.34443 <0001	-0.19981 <0001	-0.09149 0.0261	-0.04426 0.2831	-0.31370 <0001
Recruitment Process Experience					
Personableness	0.50291 <0001	-0.32094 <0001	-0.24743 <0001	-0.12195 0.0030	-0.35870 <0001
Informativeness	0.40435 <0001	-0.29078 <0001	-0.21149 <0001	-0.12784 <0.0019	-0.32707 <0001
Competence	0.52581 <0001	-0.35973 <0001	-0.26408 <0001	-0.28328 <0001	-0.39348 <0001
Previsit Information	0.33573 <0001	-0.25141 <.0001	-0.20183 <.0001	-0.19858 <.0001	-0.22528 <.0001
Applicant Treatment	0.34481 <.0001	-0.16753 <.0001	-0.15016 0.0003	-0.13486 0.0010	-0.25787 <.0001
Interview Structure	0.51240 <0001	-0.27398 <0001	-0.25472 <0001	-0.18682 <0001	-0.29393 <0001
Applicant Attractors	0.48016 <0001	-0.23881 <0001	0.18008 <0001	-0.07819 0.0579	-0.31923 <0001

It is clearly seen from table 4.10 that Commitment is significantly positively correlated with all recruitment strategy variables i.e. Information shared (r = .344), Personableness (r = .503), Informativeness (r = .404), Competence (r = .526), Previsit Information (r = .336), Applicant treatment (r = .345), Interview Structure (r= .512) and Applicant Attractors (r =.480).

Emotional Exhaustion is negatively correlated and significant with Information shared (r= -.200), Personable (r = -.321), Informativeness (r = -.290), Competence (-.360), Previsit Information (r=-.251), Applicant treatment (r = -.168), Interviewer Structure (- .274) and Applicant Attractors (r = -.239).

Personal Accomplishment is negatively correlated and significant with Information shared (r = - 0.026) Personable (r = -.247), Informativeness (r = -.211), Competence (r = -.264), Previsit Information (r = -.202), Applicant treatment (r = -.150), Interviewer Structure (r = -.255) and Applicant Attractors (r = -.180).

Depersonalization is negatively correlated and significant with Personable (r = -.122), Informativeness (r = -.128), Competence (r = -.283), Presvisit Information (r = -.199), Applicant treatment (r = -.135) and Interviewer Structure (r = -.187).

Turnover Intent is negatively correlated and significant with Information shared (r = -.314), Personable (r = -.359), Informativeness (r = -.327), Competence (r = -.393), Previsit information (r = -.225), Applicant Treatment (r = -.258), Interviewer Structure (r = -.294) and Applicant Attractors (r = -.319).

4.5 Regression Analysis

Multiple regression analysis is performed to determine the contributions of each of the specified independent variables to the variations in dependent variables.

4.5.1 Analysis of Regression: Dependent Variable - Commitment

Table 4.11 present the results of predictors of commitment. The regression coefficient of independent variables on commitment is estimated. The recruitment factors explain 42% of variation in the Commitment.

Table 4.11 - Regression Analysis – Dependent variable – Commitment

Analysis of Variance					
Source	DF	Sum of Squares	Mean Square	F Value	Pr > F
Model	9	204.80951	22.75661	45.41	<0001
Error	570	285.66383	0.50116		
Corrected Total	579	490.47335			

Root MSE	0.70793	R-Square	0.4176
Dependent Mean	4.99771	Adj R-Sq	0.4084
Coeff Var	14.16508		

Parameter Estimates						
Variable	DF	Parameter Estimate	Standard Error	t Value	Pr > |t|	Variance Inflation
Intercept	1	0.43048	0.24791	1.74	0.0830	0
Info Shared	1	0.01548	0.00470	3.29	0.0011	1.41293
Recruitment Process Experience						
Personable	1	0.20059	0.07337	2.73	0.0065	2.35667
Informativeness	1	-0.01021	0.04834	-0.21	0.8328	1.87906
Competence	1	0.35854	0.07369	4.87	<.0001	2.03564
Previsit Info	1	0.05223	0.03981	1.31	0.1901	1.31294
Appli Treatment	1	-0.7684	0.07432	-1.03	0.3016	1.58711
Intervw Structure	1	0.30503	0.07493	4.07	<.0001	2.07614
Applicant Attrtrs	1	0.27686	0.05809	4.77	<.0001	1.50108
Source	1	-0.02818	0.06066	-0.46	0.6424	1.02349

(p < 0.05, N = 591)

The relationship between information shared and commitment found to be significantly positive (β = .015, p = .001). It showed that commitment is significantly positively related to personable (β = .201, p = .007) and competence (β = .359, p = .000) factors of recruitment process. While the same show no significant relationship with informativeness (β = .010, p = .838), pre-visit information (β = .052, p = .190), and applicant treatment (β = -.077, p = .302) factors of recruitment process experience. The relationship between interview structure and commitment is significantly positive (β = .305, p = .000). The variable applicant attractor is significantly positively related to commitment (β = .277, p = .000). The relationship between recruitment source and commitment found to be statistically insignificant (β = -.028, p = .642).

Thus, at 5% level of significance null hypotheses under hypothesis numbers 4, 7, 10 and 13 are rejected, and null hypothesis under hypothesis number 1 is retained.

4.5.2 Analysis of Regression – Burnout

This section presents results of predictors of burnout. Burnout comprises three variables, namely emotional exhaustion, personal accomplishment, and depersonalization.

Analysis of Regression: Dependent Variable - Emotional Exhaustion

Table 4.12 presents the results of predictors of Emotional Exhaustion. The regression coefficient of independent variables on Emotional Exhaustion was estimated. The recruitment factors explain 17% variation in the variable Emotional Exhaustion.

Table 4.12- Regression Analysis–Dependent Variable – Emotional Exhaustion

Analysis of Variance					
Source	DF	Sum of Squares	Mean Square	F Value	Pr > F
Model	9	174.98872	19.44319	12.86	<0001
Error	570	861.56640	1.51152		
Corrected Total	579	1036.55512			

Root MSE	1.22944	R-Square	0.1688
Dependent Mean	1.58748	Adj R-Sq	0.1557
Coeff Var	77.44580		

Parameter Estimates						
Variable	DF	Parameter Estimate	Standard Error	t Value	Pr > |t|	Variance Inflation
Intercept	1	5.37628	0.43053	12.49	<.0001	0
Information Shared	1	-0.00554	0.00816	-0.68	0.4974	1.41293
Recruitment Process Experience						
Personable	1	-0.28800	0.12743	-2.26	0.0242	2.35667
Informativeness	1	-0.10339	0.08395	-1.23	0.2186	1.87906
Competence	1	-0.49823	0.12797	-3.89	0.0001	2.03564
Previsit Info	1	-0.14036	0.06914	-2.03	0.0428	1.31294
Applicant Treatment	1	0.24619	0.12907	1.91	0.0570	1.58711
Interview Structure	1	-0.11203	0.13012	-0.86	0.3896	2.07614
Applicant Attractors	1	-0.04094	0.13012	-0.86	0.3896	2.07614
Source	1	-0.03467	0.10535	-0.33	0.7422	1.02349

(p <0.05 N = 591

The recruitment process experience factors Personable (β = -.288, p = .024), Competence (β = -.498 p = .000), and Previsit

Information (β= -.140, p = .043) significantly negatively influence Emotional Exhaustion at 5% level of significance. It can be said that three factors of recruitment process experience viz. personable, competent recruitment process, and lack of previsit information influence negatively emotional exhaustion of respondents. While rest of the two factors of recruitment process experience, i.e. informativeness and applicant treatment show no significant influence on emotional exhaustion at 5% level of significance. Other variables like information shared, interview structure, applicant attractors and source are not significant at 5% level of significance in influencing Emotional exhaustion.

Analysis of Regression: Personal Accomplishment

Table 4.13 presents the results of predictors of Personal Accomplishment. The regression coefficient of independent variables on Personal accomplishment was estimated. The recruitment factors explain 9% variation in the variable Personal accomplishment.

Table 4.13 - Regression Analysis - Dependent Variable - Personal Accomplishment

Analysis of Variance					
Source	DF	Sum of Squares	Mean Square	F Value	Pr > F
Model	9	80.69920	8.96658	6.49	<.0001
Error	570	787.32179	1.38127		
Corrected Total	579	868.02098			

Root MSE	1.17527	R-Square	0.0930
Dependent Mean	1.86648	Adj R-Sq	0.0786
Coeff Var	62.96728		

Parameter Estimates						
Variable	DF	Parameter Estimate	Standard Error	t Value	Pr > |t|	Variance Inflation
Intercept	1	4.52779	0.41156	11.00	<.0001	0
Information Shared	1	0.00752	0.00780	0.96	0.3358	1.41293
Recruitment Process Experience						
Personable	1	-0.19601	0.12181	-1.61	0.1082	2.35667
Informativeness	1	-0.06338	0.08025	-0.79	0.4299	1.87906
Competence	1	-0.26741	0.12233	-2.19	0.0292	2.03564
Previsit Info	1	-0.14341	0.06610	-2.17	0.0304	1.31294
Applicant Treatment	1	0.13215	0.12339	-1.70	0.2846	0.58711
Interview Structure	1	-0.21088	0.12439	-1.70	0.0906	2.07614
Applicant Attractors	1	0.02513	0.09644	0.26	0.7945	1.50108
Source	1	0.02470	0.10071	0.25	0.8064	1.02349

(p <0.05, N = 591)

The recruitment process experience factors Competence (β = -.267, p = .029), Previsit Information (β= -.143, p = .030) significantly negatively influence Personal accomplishment at 5% level of significance. However, rest of the three factors of recruitment process experience i.e. personable, informativeness, and applicant treatment show no significant influence at 5% level of significance on personal accomplishment.

While the rest of the variables like information shared, interview structure, applicant attractors and source are not significant at 5% level of significance in influencing Personal accomplishment.

Analysis of Regression: Depersonalization

Table 4.14 presents the results of predictors of Depersonalization. The regression coefficient of independent variables on Depersonalization was estimated. The recruitment factors explain 10% variation in the variable Depersonalization.

The recruitment process experience factors Competence (β= -.607, p = .000), Previsit Information (β= -.195, p = .006) significantly negatively influence depersonalization at 5% level of significance. While rest of the three factors of recruitment process experience i.e. personable, informativeness, and applicant treatment show no significant influence on depersonalization at 5% level of significance.

Table 4.14 - Regression Analysis – Dependent Variable – Depersonalization

Analysis of Variance					
Source	DF	Sum of Squares	Mean Square	F Value	Pr > F
Model	9	96.07236	10.67471	6.86	<.0001
Error	569	885.14741	1.55562		
Corrected Total	578	981.21977			

Root MSE	1.24724	R-Square	0.0979
Dependent Mean	1.48860	Adj R-Sq	0.0836
Coeff Var	83.78637		

Parameter Estimates							
Variable	DF	Parameter Estimate	Standard Error	t Value	Pr > |t|	Variance Inflation
Intercept	1	3.77528	0.43693	8.64	<.0001	0
Information Shared	1	0.00276	0.00829	0.33	0.7397	1.41360
Recruitment Process Experience						
Personable	1	0.10259	0.12929	0.79	0.4278	2.35688
Informativeness	1	0.00960	0.08519	0.11	0.9103	1.87953
Competence	1	-0.60668	0.12983	-4.67	<0001	2.03508
Previsit Info	1	-0.19479	0.07016	-2.78	0.0057	1.31306
Applicant Treatment	1	0.06774	0.13094	0.52	0.6051	1.58701
Interview Structure	1	-0.19717	0.13203	-1.49	0.1359	2.07551
Applicant Attractors	1	0.19872	0.10235	1.94	0.0527	1.50097
Source	1	-0.01082	0.10699	-0.10	0.9194	1.02312

(p <0.05, N = 591)

Remaining variables like information shared, interview structure, applicant attractors, and source are not significant at 5% level of significance in influencing Depersonalization.

Thus, at 5% level of significance null hypothesis under hypothesis number 8 is rejected, and null hypotheses under hypothesis numbers 2, 5, 11, and 14 are retained.

4.5.3 Analysis of Regression: Turnover Intent

Table 4.15 presents the results of predictors of Turnover intent. The regression coefficient of independent variables on Turnover intent was estimated. The recruitment factors explain 23% variation in the variable Turnover intent.

Table 4.15 - Regression Analysis- Dependent Variable – Turnover Intent

Analysis of Variance					
Source	DF	Sum of Squares	Mean Square	F Value	Pr > F
Model	9	124.76719	13.86302	18.71	<.0001
Error	570	422.27920	0.74084		
Corrected Total	579	547.04640			

Root MSE	0.86072	R-Square	0.2281
Dependent Mean	2.77362	Adj R-Sq	0.2159
Coeff Var	31.03240		

Parameter Estimates						
Variable	DF	Parameter Estimate	Standard Error	t Value	Pr > |t|	Variance Inflation
Intercept	1	5.9357	0.30141	19.69	<.0001	0
Information Shared	1	-0.02235	0.00572	-3.91	0.0001	1.41293
Recruitment Process Experience						
Personable	1	-0.10617	0.08921	-1.19	0.2345	2.35667
Informativeness	1	-0.04748	0.05877	-0.81	0.4195	1.87906
Competence	1	-0.40498	0.08959	-4.52	<.0001	2.03564
Previsit Info	1	0.00181	0.04841	0.04	0.9701	1.31294
Applicant Treatment	1	-0.05658	0.09036	-0.63	0.5314	1.58711
Interview Structure	0	0.03259	0.09110	0.36	0.7206	2.07614
Applicant Attractors	1	-0.18205	0.07063	-2.58	0.0102	1.50108
Source	1	0.07827	0.07375	1.06	0.2890	1.02349

($p < 0.05$, N = 591

Results of this study show that information shared (β = -.022, p = .000) significantly negatively influence turnover intent at 5% level of significance. Factor Competence (β = -.405, p = .000) of recruitment process experience has significantly negative influence on turnover intent at 5% level of significance. Similarly, applicant attractors (β = -.182, p = .010) negatively influence turnover intent at 5% level of significance.

While no significant influence of three recruitment process experience factors i.e. personable, informativeness, pre-visit information; and applicant treatment, interview structure, source is seen on turnover intent at 5% level of significance.

Thus, null hypotheses under hypothesis numbers 6, 9, and 15 are rejected, and null hypotheses under hypothesis numbers 3 and 12 are retained at 5% level of significance.

4.6 Summary of Regression Analysis and Hypotheses Testing

In the preceding sections, regression analysis is performed by splitting two variables, namely recruitment process experience, and burnout for detailed understanding. If we combine these variables the information may be lost. The summary of the entire regression analysis is presented in table 4.16.

Table 4.16- Summary of Regression Analysis

Independent/Dependent Variable	Commitment	Burnout				Turnover Intent
		Emotional Exhaustion	Personal Accomplishment	Depersonalization	Combined Burnout	
Information shared*	S	NS	NS	NS	NS	S
Recruitment process Experience*	S	S	S	S	S	S
Personable**	S	S	NS	NS	S	NS
Informativeness**	NS	NS	NS	NS	NS	NS
Competence**	S	S	S	S	S	S
Previsit Information**	NS	S	S	S	S	NS
Applicant treatment**	NS	NS	NS	NS	NS	NS
Interview structure*	S	NS	NS	NS	NS	NS
Applicant attractors*	S	NS	NS	NS	NS	S
Source*	NS	NS	NS	NS	NS	NS

(S = Significant, NS = Not Significant, * = Variables, ** = Factors)

If at least one of the components of the variables is significant, then that variable can be considered as significantly correlated or significantly influencing dependent variable. Considering the same, hypotheses testing can be summarized in table 4.17.

Table 4.17 - Summary of Hypotheses Testing

H No.	Null Hypotheses	Results
1	There is no significant relationship between recruitment sources and committed employees retained in the organization.	Retained
2	There is no significant relationship between recruitment sources and burnout employees in the organization.	Retained
3	There is no significant relationship between recruitment sources and turnover intention of employee	Retained
4	There is no significant relationship between information shared and committed employees in the organization.	Rejected
5	There is no significant relationship between information shared and burnout employees in the organization.	Retained
6	There is no significant relationship between information shared and turnover intention of employees.	Rejected
7	There is no significant relationship between recruiter and recruitment process and committed employees in the organization	Rejected
8	There is no significant relationship between recruiter and recruitment process and burnout employees in the organization.	Rejected
9	There is no significant relationship between recruiter and recruitment process and turnover intention of employees.	Rejected
10	There is no significant relationship between interview structure and committed employees in the organization.	Rejected
11	There is no significant relationship between interview structure and burnout employees in the organization.	Retained
12	There is no significant relationship between interview structure and turnover intention of employees.	Retained
13	There is no significant relationship between applicant attractors and committed employees in the organization.	Rejected
14	There is no significant relationship between applicant attractors and burnout employees in the organization.	Retained
15	There is no significant relationship between applicant attractors and turnover intention of employees.	Rejected

4.7 Discussion

The present study examined relation and influence of elements of recruitment strategy on employee retention in Indian banking and insurance sector. The current study shows that most of the elements of recruitment strategy (for e.g. information shared, recruitment process experience, interview structure, and applicant attractors) influence organizational commitment of employees. Whereas, only one element of recruitment strategy i.e. recruitment process experience influences burnout among the employees. It is also seen in the current study that few elements of recruitment strategy (i.e. information shared, recruitment process experience, and applicant attractors) influence turnover intent among employees in Indian banking and insurance sector.

The results show no significant relationship between recruitment source and commitment. This is in congruence with the findings of Saks (1994) contending that there is no difference in organizational commitment of employees in relation to the source of recruitment. However, Aamodt and Carr (1988) and Wanous (1992) concluded that recruiting employees via referrals and internal sources results in slightly higher job survival than other sources of recruitment. The differential effectiveness of various sources of recruitment may be a function of the realism found within the information available relating to the vacancy (Wanous, 1980). Therefore, the sources like referrals and internal sources give more information to the candidate about the job, and company to make a decision. Further, it leads to higher rate of job survival and commitment. Moser (2005) found that unmet expectations mediated the relation between type of recruitment source (internal vs. external) and organizational commitment. Moser conducted this study among the engineers who newly joined one electric company. Employees with not more than 32 months of experience in the current organization were considered by him. The results of the present study might be different as the present study is for different sectors viz. bank and insurance companies that too in Indian context.

Results of regression analysis show that recruitment source is insignificant in influencing burnout of employees in organizations studied. The results are different than the findings of Quaglieri (1982) and Schwab (1982) who contended that some recruitment source can be effectively related to various organizational criteria. Current study has considered respondents with certain number of years of experience in the industry. Therefore, for the employees with previous experience, source of recruitment might be the least important as compared to the other factors of recruitment.

The present study also shows difference in the results of the studies conducted by Gannon (1971), Decker & Cornelius (1979), and Breaugh (1981) who found that informal recruiting source produce superior new hires relative to hires recruited via formal sources. Breaugh (1981) further supported the argument that those recruited via newspaper advertisements lost almost twice as many days as those recruited through other sources. This absenteeism might be because of high level of stress or burnout in the organization. Latham & Leddy (1987) further reported that employees hired through referrals are more satisfied compared to employees hired through newspaper advertisement. The present study has considered different operational definition of source i.e. source as internal and external source of recruitment. This might be the reason for the difference in the results of previous studies and the current study.

As per analysis of the present study, recruitment source is not significant in influencing turnover intent among the respondents studied. The results are similar to the results of William, Labig, and Stone (1993) who conducted study among nurses, did not find recruitment source having effects on employee turnover. Similarly, a study by Swaroff et al. (1985) failed to find recruitment source effects on turnover among technical salespersons.

Cardiello (2002) also found that source of recruitment is not significant in influencing participants' intention to stay with the organization.

Whereas, few researcher have reported different results. Kirnan (1986) found that informal sources have higher survival rates than formal sources of recruitment. Aamodt and Carr (1986), Breaugh & Mann (1984), and Conard & Ashworth (1986) contended employee referrals give longest tenure followed by walk-ins, employment agencies, and advertisements. Results of study by Ullman (1966) show that employees recruited via informal sources had a lower turnover rate than employees recruited via formal sources. Gannon (1971), Taylor and Schmidt (1983) too depicted through their study the relationship between employee referrals and turnover. Taylor & Schmidt (1983) conducted study among the workers who were hired for seasonal work. Therefore, we can see that for short tenure of work, referral is important to avoid turnover of employees. But in case of long tenure jobs the same may not be true. Similarly, Decker & Cornelius (1979) speculated that individuals recruited via newspaper advertisements or employment agencies might be more prone to quitting the job. Sommerville (1996) who conducted study among construction employees concluded that each organization studied demonstrated sources which are shown to be associated with high levels of employee turnover. The results might differ depending on the type of organization. The realism aspect of source suggests that individuals recruited via sources which provide more accurate information will be able to self-select out of jobs which do not meet their needs. Therefore, subsequent turnover will be less for employees recruited by means of more informative sources (Breaugh & Mann, 1984).

The studies reviewed by Zottoli & Wanous (2000) do not provide a clear consensus as to which explanation for recruitment source effectiveness is most credible. We can also see that most of the recruitment source studies that were conducted till 80's show significant influence of source on employee reactions in terms of commitment, burnout, and turnover intent. Studies that were conducted after 90's show no significant influence of source on employee reactions. Thus, we may say that after the development of internet, job sites, information revolution, source of recruitment per se may not have significance as compared to other elements of recruitment.

The relationship between information shared and commitment found to be significantly positive. The findings are similar to the findings of Wanous (1973) who contended that realistic job preview or information given to the candidates during recruitment results in their commitment. Phillips (1998) revealed moderating effects of timing of realistic job preview on increased loyalty amongst employees. Rynes (1989) too hypothesized that people develop stronger commitment to the organizations that give them the information they need to make fully informed job choices. Stiff (1994) believed that trustworthy information during recruitment impacted job survival. Similarly, Roberson et al. (2005) found that recruitment information specificity influences candidates' attraction to organization. Thus, present study has confirmed results of the studies mentioned above in Indian banking and insurance sector. We may conclude that when essential information shared by the organization is specific and shared on time, it influences commitment of the employees.

In this present study, no significant relationship is found between information shared and burnout. The results are dissimilar to the results of Wanous (1973) who concluded that accurate and complete information given to candidates leads to increased satisfaction. Schneider (1976) believed that organizations oversell vacancies or inflate information to candidates at the expense of employee satisfaction. Similarly, after considering

40 studies Phillips (1998) revealed moderate effects of timing of information shared and job satisfaction. A meta analysis by Chapman & Webster (2006) as well as Rynes, Bretz & Gerhart (1991) have found that longer delays in communication during recruitment leads to negative perceptions of the organization. Rynes, Bretz, & Grehart (1991) have considered 41 graduating students for their study. The results may differ when the study is conducted among working professionals. People who are unhappy in their jobs may blame that unhappiness on having had inadequate or inaccurate information before they accepted offer rather than on poor personal decision making. It is also possible that individuals who are relatively dissatisfied will selectively recall information or distort it to show that they got inaccurate pictures of jobs. Thus, we may say that information shared during recruitment process needs to be accurate and adequate.

Results of this study show significantly negative relationship between information shared and turnover intent. The results are similar to the findings of various other researchers. Caldwell and O'Reilly (1985) found in their study that individuals who report that they have received accurate information about jobs are less likely to leave their organizations than those who have received inaccurate information. Though the sample for their study was MBA graduates, we found similar results. Becker et al. (2010) found that timing in the final phases of recruitment and selection impacts recruitment outcome including employee turnover. Meyer et al, (2003) emphasised that information shared at the time of recruitment function as realistic job preview reduces turnover. Similarly, Phillips (1998), Breaugh (1992), Dean & Wanous (1984), Quaglieri (1982), Reilly et al. (1981), Schneider (1976), and Wanous (1973) also found negative relationship between information shared and turnover among employees. Briefly we can say that according to socialization theory, information shared by the organization as a part of socialization tactics help embed the individual into the organization and reduce turnover (Allen, 2006). This suggests that when individuals choose jobs using accurate information, their decisions are better than if they use artificially positive or inaccurate information.

The results of analysis show significantly positive relationship between recruitment process and commitment. Recruitment process is further analyzed after splitting the same into five factors. It showed that commitment is significantly positively related to personable and competence factors of recruitment process. While the same show no significant relationship with informativeness, pre-visit information, and applicant treatment factors. The results are similar to the findings of Rynes & Miller (1983) and Harris & Fink (1987) which showed that recruiter characteristics were significantly related to regard for company. They considered personableness as important characteristics of recruiter. As predicted by both the studies, current research also shows that recruitment process experience is more important in the field setting than in the laboratory context.

As per Kreisman (2002) commitment is the result of complex conditions stimulated by a variety of corporate actions and those actions often are first experienced by employees during the recruiting process. Rynes, Heneman, & Schwab (1980), Schmitt & Coyle (1976) have contended that applicants form strong impressions of organizational recruiters. These impressions often affect how applicants approach subsequent steps of the recruitment process (Harris & Fink, 1987; Rynes, Bretz, & Gerhart, 1991). Schmitt and Coyle (1976) contended that recruiter's characteristics and presentation are related to the likelihood of the applicant accepting employment. Therefore, competence of the recruitment process plays important role in creating positive influence on applicant.

Current analysis shows that recruitment process is significantly negatively related to burnout. The components of recruitment process and burnout clearly depict the relationship. The results show that recruitment process factors personable, competence, and pre-visit information, showed significantly negative relationship with emotional exhaustion. Informativeness and applicant treatment show no significant relationship with emotional exhaustion.

Competence and pre-visit information factors are significantly negatively related to personal accomplishment. While there is no significant relationship found between personable, informativeness, applicant treatment and personal accomplishment.

Results show that competence and pre-visit information significantly negatively related to depersonalization. While there is no significant relationship found between personable, informativeness, applicant treatment and depersonalization. Researchers (e.g., Connerley & Rynes, 1997) have suggested that recruiter personableness may be important because it "signals" how the person may be treated if hired or how likely the person is to receive a job offer. Connerley & Rynes (1997) conducted study among the students appearing for campus interview. Similar results are seen in the study where personableness is significantly negatively related to emotional exhaustion.

In the present study, recruitment process show significantly negative relationship with turnover intent. Competence factor of recruitment process is significantly negatively related to turnover intent. While no significant relationship is found between personable, informativeness, pre-visit information, applicant treatment, and turnover intent. The results are similar to the findings of Fields (2001) who posted that an organization may have the most elaborate and sophisticated recruitment program, but once individuals are hired; if the environment is inhospitable then companies will soon find themselves looking for another replacement due to turnover of employees. Taylor & Bergmann (1987) found that candidates may voluntarily withdraw from consideration in response to aversive recruitment activities such as inconsiderate treatment during recruitment process. These were pre-hire reactions of the candidates who were students undergoing recruitment activities. Once candidates are hired, the treatment given to them during recruitment process may become insignificant for deciding their intention to leave the organization. Perceptions of procedural justice during recruitment have been shown to relate to organizationally valued outcomes, such as job satisfaction, commitment, turnover, and performance (Robertson et al. 1991; Konovsky & Cropanzano, 1991). Buck and Watson (2002) further supported the interconnection between recruitment and retention saying that using appropriate recruitment processes actually reduced employee turnover.

Liden & Parsons (1986) and Harris & Fink (1987) contended that the recruiter's personableness, as well as how informative he or she was, influenced the applicants affect toward the job. While, present study does not show any such relationships between informativeness on one hand and commitment, burnout or turnover intent on the other. Most of the studies related to recruitment are done in college settings and campus recruitment contexts. The results might be different because present study is conducted on employees as a sample rather than college students.

Current study supports psychological contracts theory. According to psychological contract theory the recruitment process is for the parties (i.e. recrtuiter and candidates) to negotiate a "psychological contract" (Herriot, 1989). Employees who perceive that their employer fulfills its obligations are more likely to become more engaged and are less likely to leave the organization (Rousseau, 1995).

As per current analysis the relationship between interview structure and commitment is significantly positive. The recruitment interviewer influences employees in the long term in the form of their commitment to the organization. It may be accepted that interviewers attract right candidates and persuade them to accept job offer (Alderfer & McCord, 1970; Schmitt, 1976; Schmitt & Coyle, 1976). Campion et al. (1998) also strongly recommended use of structured interviews over unstructured interviews.

The results of present study do not show any significant relationship between interview structure and burnout. Burnout factors give detailed information on analysis. It has been found in the present study that there is no significant relationship between interview structure and emotional exhaustion, personal accomplishment, and depersonalization. Different results are reported by Jablin & McComb (1984) and Herriot (1988, 1989), who proposed that interview can be seen as an information, expectation and perception exchange event. According to Schmitt and Coyle (1976), a combination of the interviewer's empathetic behaviour, preparation, and ability to supply information was predictive of the candidate's perception of his/her performance and degree of favourability towards a company. Herriot (1988) as well as Schmitt & Coyle (1976) conducted their studies among graduating students. The results may be different if the same is conducted among working professionals. We may also say that the results of interview structure might affect candidates immediately after or during interview. But once the interview is over in the long run it might be something other than interview structure that influence the burnout of employees.

The regression analysis in present study shows that there is no significant relationship between interview structure and turnover intent. The structure of interview, content of interview, and behaviour of interviewer during interview do not influence turnover intention of employees. The results are against the findings of Schmidt & Rader (1999) who found that structured employment interview can predict employee turnover. After review of 200 articles and books Campion et al. (1998) concluded that structuring the interview enhances its reliability and validity, and hence its usefulness for prediction and decision making. We may say that in the long run factors other than recruitment interview influences turnover intent among employees of the organization.

The variable applicant attractor is significantly positively related to commitment. The results are similar to the finding of Weiss (1980) and Yellen (1984) who suggested that enhanced applicant attractors have positive impact on the quality as well quantity of those attracted to and retained by organizations. Similarly, various applicant attractors, such as training, compensation, and advancement opportunities, have been found to have positive effects on applicant attraction to firms (Powell, 1984; Taylor & Bergmann, 1987). Collins & Stevens (2002) and Slaughter et al. (2004) contended that strong employer brand attracts better applicants. As per the views of Rynes et al. (1980) both theoretical and empirical works have suggested that variation in attraction practices can have important effects on long-term outcomes as well.

No significant relationship is seen in the present study between applicant attractors and burnout. Applicant attractor is not seen to be significantly related to emotional exhaustion, personal accomplishment, and depersonalization. We can say that other than applicant attractors, factors affect burnout level of employees in the long term. Studies by Rynes (1991) and Gatewood, et al. (1993) suggested that applicant attractor factors may affect recruitment outcomes by affecting applicants' perceptions and application decisions during the initial phase of recruitment. As the applicant attraction strategy is aimed at attracting candidates to apply to the positions in the organization, it does not show significant influence on burnout of employees.

The current results show that applicant attractor is significantly negatively related to turnover intent. When organizations make use of applicant attractor factors during recruitment process it influences the image of organization in the minds of applicants which leads to lower turnover intention among them. It is evident from the results of the study by Shah & Bharati (2014) that individuals do not join an insurance company only for fair compensation and employment; instead they also look for job security, ease of working in flexible timing, and career advancement. Studies by Hamlet (1989) and Lakhani (1988) showed that enhanced applicant attractors lead to reduced turnover amongst the employees. Even Turban and Cable (2003) found positive links between applicant attractors and organization-level recruitment outcomes.

Majority of previous research has been conducted in college placement offices and has focused college graduates (e.g. Breaugh 1992, Rynes, 1991). Thus, it becomes difficult to generalize previous findings. Breaugh (1992) has further argued that it is crucially important for recruitment researchers to expand their investigations beyond the college placement office. This study has considered professionals working with banks and insurance companies in India with at least one year of experience in the industry.

From the descriptive statistics we may say that employees in banking and insurance sector found recruitment process to be highly personable, informative, and competent, with required pre-visit information shared to them along with fair treatment at the time of recruitment. The interviews are highly structured in Indian banking and insurance sector. The employees are found to be attracted to the banks and insurance companies' attractor factors like salary, benefits, career growth opportunities, training, good geographic locations, etc. The employees in Indian banking and insurance sector are seen to be highly committed to their organizations. While at the same time they show moderate level of intention to leave the organization.

As per the results of this study, female employees show comparatively higher level of commitment to the organization than male employees. This might be because female employees are willing to do a lot for their job status. It is seen in the study that male employees show higher turnover intent that female employees. This might be because male employees are more interested in continuously higher pay package, designation, and career growth etc.

It is also seen in the current study that employees below 25 years of age show higher level of commitment compared to other age groups studied. As till 25 years of age employees try to settle in a job and understand the work, therefore, they might show higher level of commitment than those in other age groups. Employees of age groups of 35-45 years in Indian banking and insurance sector show highest level of turnover intention. This might be because employees between age groups 35-45 years are seen to be changing jobs frequently. The reason of change in job might be good pay package, career growth, etc.

The current study also shows that employees with qualification other than traditional degree show higher level of commitment to organization than that of other employees. The types of other qualifications in this study include specific courses developed for banking employees and certain insurance related certifications. As these employees have specific work related knowledge, they might show higher level of commitment than employees with traditional degrees. It is seen from the results of the current study that employees with master degree show higher level of intention to leave. This might be because the employees with master degree think that they deserve better job profile in some other organizations.

The results of the current study show that employees having less than 12 months of experience in the current organization show highest level of commitment. The reason for this commitment might be that they want to understand the job well, get more knowledge in the area of work. The intention to leave is highest among the employees with 3-5 years of experience in the current organization. The reason for intention to leave among employees with 3-5 years of experience in the current organization might be that they get saturated in the same organization and they need change in the same.

Whereas, the total experience in the banking and insurance sector is concerned it is seen in the present study that employees with total experience of less than 12 months in the banking and insurance sector show highest level of commitment. Again the reason might be that they are new in the banking and insurance sector and they try to understand the way of working in the sector and they try to get hands on knowledge. The employees with 3-5 years of total experience in the banking and insurance sector show highest level of turnover intent. This might be because they want to work with other similar organizations; the chances of growth are less in the current organization, etc.

The present study shows that employees working at top managerial positions in the Indian banking and insurance sector show highest level of commitment. In most of the organizations, performance of the top level managers is linked to the performance of the organization. These top level managers possess good experience in the industry as well as in their own organization. This might be the reason for their commitment towards the organization. The intention to leave the organization is highest among employees at middle management level. The middle management level employees are prone to poaching by other organizations in the sector. The employees themselves are often on the lookout for higher pay scale and career growth. This might be the reason for their intention to leave the organization.

The current study depicts that the employees in co-operative banks show highest level of commitment. Co-operative banks are community based organizations. The reason for commitment among employees might be their view that they are doing community work and the growth of the organization will lead to growth of their community. Among various types of banks (co-operative banks, private sector banks, and foreign banks) and insurance companies (private insurance companies and foreign insurance companies) private sector bank employees show highest level of intention to leave the organization. The market offers wide choice of higher designations and pay package. They can also move to insurance companies and other financial institutions. Therefore, there might be the highest level of intention to leave among private bank employees.

Based on the analysis of data and discussion, conclusions are drawn. These conclusions are presented in the next chapter. The next chapter also gives implications of study as well as suggestions for further research.

CHAPTER V

CONCLUSION, IMPLICATIONS AND SUGGESTIONS FOR FURTHER RESEARCH

5.1 Chapter Overview

This chapter describes major conclusions of the study. It states implications of the study to academics as well as to the industry. This chapter concludes with suggestions for further research.

5.2 Conclusions

Well defined and well executed recruitment strategy yields reliable results and can be a competitive advantage in the war for talent. Key employee retention is critical to the long term health and success of any business. The results of this study are supportive of the existence of significant relationships between a set of independent variables and employee retention. It is evident from this study that all recruitment strategy variables except source of recruitment individually show significant correlation with post-hire outcomes of retention like commitment, burnout, and turnover intent.

We agree with the results by Punia and Sharma (2008) who say that if companies want to keep up with their competition, they have to find the right people and understand how to find people who will be committed to the company. There are no short cuts in finding long-term, quality employees. In terms of recruitment, companies should therefore put emphasis on not only considering formal qualifications, evaluating job relevant technical ability, etc., but also share right information to the candidate at right time, give positive recruitment experience, fair interview structure, and execute realistic applicant attractors.

This study adds to literature on recruitment and retention in several ways. Firstly, as per the available research literature, the present study is one of the initial attempts to explore empirically the effects of various elements of recruitment strategy together on retention.

Secondly, most of the previous research was conducted in college setting focusing fresh graduates in recruitment process, whereas the current study has considered professionals already working with banks and insurance companies for at least one year.

Thirdly, it validates two theories i.e. organizational justice theory and, person- perception theory. These two theories show link between recruitment practices and applicants' reactions to the recruitment. According to organizational justice theory, which has taken form of 'procedural justice theory', the candidates perceive and judge the selection process in terms of fairness, that is, satisfaction or violation of a set of specific procedural rules. Perceptions of procedural justice during recruitment have been shown to relate to outcomes, such as organizational commitment.

The second attempt to theoretically link recruitment practices with candidates' reactions comes from the person-perception theory. Earlier in this thesis it was stated that one of the aims of the recruitment process is for both the parties (i.e. interviewers and candidates) to negotiate a "psychological contract". This can be done either by explicitly stating each party's expectations or, by assuming and inferring them.

Applicants believe in the information shared by the organization at various stages of recruitment. They consider this information credible and develop interest in the organization. Results of this study show that sharing required information in a realistic, specific manner and on time is essential for influencing commitment of employees and the same will help organizations to avoid their turnover intentions.

Providing a realistic picture of the role and work profile, potential future career opportunities, working conditions, brief information about co-workers, and level of responsibility in the organization as well as training and development opportunities, will help employees make fully informed choices, and develop commitment as also minimize attrition among them. Such information can be shared by the organization at various stages, for example, through advertisement of vacancy, during interview, etc.

Candidates can get this information from their friends working in the organization, recruiter, interviewer, or through newspaper, trade magazines, and from internet. One of the most important sources of information about an organization is the organization itself. Developing and sharing realistic as well as specific information is relatively inexpensive, and the returns, even in small effects, can be great in terms of lower recruitment and turnover cost.

The overall recruitment process experience creates impressions of organization on candidates. Employees get signals of unknown organizational attributes during recruitment process. These impressions eventually affect the level of commitment, burnout, and turnover intentions of employees. Personableness of the organization (e.g. caring and empathetic) during recruitment influences the commitment of employees while the same can help in reducing emotional exhaustion among them. It may be because personableness of the recruiter organization signals how the applicant will be treated, if hired.

Recruiting competence of the organization plays vital role in influencing employees' commitment. Competence of handling recruitment process effectively, ability to answer candidates' questions is expected by the candidates during recruitment process. It also has negative influence on burnout and turnover intention amongst them. Thus, it is important for the organization to concentrate on creating competent recruitment process to avoid feelings of burnout and intention to leave among employees.

As a part of recruitment process organization is supposed to share pre-visit information like place as well as time of visit and receiving persons at the time of visit to the organization. Lack of such information during recruitment influences burnout amongst the employees. It can be concluded here that creating personable, competent recruitment process with clear pre-visit information will help organization to influence commitment of employees, their feeling of burnout, and intention to leave the organization. This will require little efforts from the recruiters, but results will be remarkable in terms of employee retention.

Candidates' experience with interviewer and interview structure during recruitment has its influence on commitment of the employees. Structured interviews considering topics discussed during interview, information provided, interviewer's ability to control interview, his/her willingness to listen to the interviewees, giving opportunity to applicant for an effective self-presentation, and knowledge of the content of the application form play important role in influencing commitment of employees. Such interviews do not play any role in influencing burnout and turnover intention among them.

Interviews can be structured by making interviewer more informed about the vacant job and candidate information, interviewer can allow candidates to ask questions during the interview, he should be able to control the interview process, and also include variety of questions related to candidate and job profile. Interviews can be structured in many different ways and its components are easy to implement. So, there seems to be little reason not to structure interviews.

Applicant attractor factors positively influence employee commitment. Applicant attractor factors like good starting salary, employee benefits, job security, training and development practices of organization, career growth opportunities, good management philosophy, reputation of the organization, and good geographic location options play important role in influencing employees.

When applicant attractors are extensively used by the organization in recruiting employees and later fulfilled them, it helps organization to influence employee commitment in a positive manner. But, if the same is not fulfilled it leads to intention of turnover among employees. Therefore, organizations should make careful use of attractor factors while designing their recruitment strategy.

Recruitment source is not significant in influencing commitment, burnout parameters or turnover intention among employees studied. When employees stay with the organization for more than a year, as in case of this study, for them other factors are more important than source of their recruitment. Factors like information shared during recruitment, recruitment process experience, interview structure, and applicant attractors used by the organization become more important than source of their recruitment. Previous research mentioned in the literature considered source as a source of information and its influence on employee reactions. While current study has considered only source of recruitment, which has come out to be insignificant in influencing employee retention. But, information shared seems to be significant in influencing employee retention.

The relationship between elements of recruitment strategy (except recruitment process) and burnout being not significant, suggest that measures of recruitment must be combined with other measures to effectively predict and understand burnout. No organization knowingly hires employees who intend to quit, but separating truth from fiction during the selection process is an enormous challenge. It is well known that the Indian environment does not offer abundant and equal opportunity in all categories of employment to give a meaningful interpretation to employee commitment, burnout, and turnover intention. Thus, leaving and staying with the organization is not necessarily a function of only recruitment strategy in Indian organizations. There are several other factors involved like work environment, supervisor, co-workers, economic development of the country as well as growth of the industry.

The overall banking and insurance sector in India is very optimistic about the future based on the economic hopefulness and projections. The current study is one of the serious efforts to arrest employee retention, which might have a direct bearing on the growth and financials of the companies.

5.3 Implications

Present study suggests few implications for both practitioners and future researchers. This study is an attempt to look into recruitment strategy and process in line with suggestions given by Sara Rynes (1989). She states that future research should consider the way recruitment activities lead to recruitment processes, and how the same affects recruitment outcomes.

This study has important implications for the practice of recruitment and employee retention. Practitioners can improve their recruitment strategy considering its retention effects. Effectively, recruitment is 'buying' an employee (price being the salary multiplied by probable years of service). Hence, bad buys can be very expensive. According to a Harvard Business Review (cited in Yager, 2012), 80 percent of employee turnover is due to hiring mistakes. Employee turnover, and thereafter replacement, and training costs are estimated to be 1.5 to 2.5 times of annual salary for each person who quits. Retention strategies should not be orchestrated in isolation but must form part of the overall strategies for strengthening the pull on the talent, which in fact include sourcing, staffing and development strategies. In order to improve the accuracy of such decision, systematic and scientific procedure for recruitment should be followed. And therefore, it becomes essential for the organizations to adopt such recruitment strategy that helps them retain employees in the organization for longer tenure, strategy that helps them avoid people who might get into burnout mode, or who might intend to leave the organization.

Kundu & Malhan (2009) stated in their study that recruitment is moderately practiced in Indian insurance companies. Indian banks and insurance companies should consider each element of recruitment strategy carefully for its retention effect.

Organizations should consider recruitment as a two way process and realize that both applicants and organizations make decisions in the process. Organization should not underestimate the power of information shared during recruitment. Sharing enough recruitment information at right time will result in positive response from the employees. Organizations should take proactive steps in improving recruitment process. Recruitment process that is personable, well informed, competent, with required pre-visit information, and fair treatment to applicants influences commitment of employees and their intention to leave the organization. Thus, good amount of time and efforts need to be invested for effective recruitment process. Interviews should be highly structured. Structured interview help in gaining commitment of employees and reduces their intention to leave the organization.

Recruiting the best staff has always been an important measure of organizational success. In simple words, organizations should attract right pool of candidates for selection, add value to recruitment and interview process, heighten employee loyalty, and improve retention rates simultaneously. It can be concluded that when an organization's talent management process evolves in the manner described in this section, organizations will be reluctant to follow any stop-gap measures of recruiting and retention.

5.4 Suggestions for Further Research

This study investigated banking and insurance sector in India, further study is advocated to understand how recruitment strategy and employee retention, and their linkages vary among other sectors. This will also help in developing a model to test recruitment strategy and employee retention.

This study is cross-sectional in design. Future research extended to the use of longitudinal designs is strongly recommended.

Given the tremendous growth in the recruitment research it will be of considerable advantage if standardized measures are developed for recruitment strategy. Different researchers have used different factor structures and different construct names. It can be standardized by repeating this study with different respondents and different contexts.

BIBLIOGRAPHY

Aamodt, M. G., & Carr, K. (1988). Relationship between recruitment source and employee behavior. Paper presented at the Annual Meeting of the International Personnel Management Association and Assessment Council, Las Vegas, NV, 1988, June.

Abbasi, S.M., and Hollman K. (2000). Turnover : the real bottom line. *Public Personnel Management.* Retrieved October6, 2006, from http://www.findarticles.com/p/articles/mi_qa3779/is_200010/ai_n8926885

Ackoff, R. (1970). A concept of corporate planning. New York Wiley.

Ackoff, R. (1974). Redesigning the future. New York Wiley.

Adamsky, H. (2005). 6 Ways recruiters can support building a better organization: initiatives to focus on in the coming year. Web document: URL: *www.erexchange.com*.

Adkins, C. (1995). "Previous Work Experience and Organizational Socialization: A Longitudinal Examination." *Academy of Management Journal ^8:* 839-862.

Ahuja, M., Katherine M., George, J., Kacmar, C., McKnight, H. (2002). Overworked and Isolated? Predicting the Effect of Work-family Conflict, Autonomy, and Workload on Organizational Commitment and Turnover of Virtual Workers. Proceedings of the 35th Hawaii International Conference on System Sciences.

Ajzen, I. and Fishbein, M. (1980), Understanding Attitudes and Predicting Social Behavior, Prentice Hall, Englewood Cliffs, NJ.

Alderfer, C.P. and McCord, C.G. (1970). Personal and situational factors in the recruitment interview. *Journal of Applied Psychology*, Vol. 54, pp. 377-85.

Alexander, J.A., Bloom, J.R., and Nichols, B.A. (1994). Nursing turnover and hospital efficiency: An organizational-level analysis. *Industrial Relations, 33*, 505-520.

Alexander, J.A., Lichtenstein, R., Oh, H.J. and Ullman, E. (1998). A causal model of voluntary turnover among nursing personnel in long-term psychiatric settings. *Research in Nursing and Health*, Vol. 21, pp. 415-27.

Allen, D. G. (2006). "Do Organizational Socialization Tactics Influence Newcomer Embeddedness and Turnover?" *Journal of Management* 32: 237-256.

Allen, N.J. and Meyer, J.P. (1990). The measurement and antecedents of affective, continuance and normative commitment to the organization. *Journal of Occupational Psychology, 63*, 1 – 18.

Almer, E., Kaplan, S.E. (2002). The effects of flexible work arrangements on stressors, burnout, and behavioral job outcomes in public accounting. *Behavioral Research in Accounting,* Vol. 14, 2002.

Amundson, N. (2007). The influence of workplace attraction on recruitment and retention. Journal of Employment Counselling. Volume 44.

Angle, H. and Perry, J. (1981). An empirical assessment of organizational commitment and organizational effectiveness. *Administrative Science Quarterly, 26*, 1-14.

Armitage, C.J. and Connor, M. (2001). Efficacy of the theory of planned behavior: a meta-analytic review. *British Journal of Social Psychology*, Vol. 40, pp. 471-99.

Arnold, H. J., and Feldman D. C. (1982). A multivariate analysis of the determinants of job turnover. *Journal of Applied Psychology.* Vol.67, No. 3, pg. 350-360.

Arthur, J. B. (1994). Effects of human resource systems on manufacturing performance and turnover. Academy of Management, 37, 670–687.

Arvey, R. D., and Champion, J. E. (1982). The employment interview: A summary review of the present research. *Personnel Psychology.* 35, 281-322.

Baack, D., Luthans, F., and Rogers, J. (1993). Analysis of the organizational commitment of clergy members. *Journal of Managerial Issues, 5*, 232-253.

Balaji, C. (1986). Toward a new measure of organizational commitment. *Indian Journal of Industrial Relations.* Vol. 21, No.3.

Balfour, D. L. and Wechsler, B. (1994). A theory of public sector commitment: Towards a reciprocal model of person and organization. In J. Perry (Ed.), Research in Public Administration, 3: 281-314. Greenwich, CT: JAI Press.

Bamberger, P and Meshoulam, I. (2000). Human resource strategy: Formulation, implementation, and impact. *Sage Publications, Inc., pg. 5-6.*

Barber AE. (1998). *Recruiting employees: Individual and organizational perspectives.* Thousand Oaks, CA: Sage.

Barber, A.E., Hollenbeck, J.R., Tower, S.L. and Phillips, J.M. (1994). The effects of interview focus on recruitment effectiveness: a field experiment. *Journal of Applied Psychology*, Vol. 79, 1994, pp. 886-96.

Barney, J. (1991). Firm resources and sustained competitive advantage. *Journal of Management*, 17, 99–120.

Barney, J. B. (2001a). Is the resource-based view a useful perspective for strategic management research? Yes. *Academy of Management Review*, 26, 41–56.

Barney, J., Wright, M., & Ketchen Jr., D. J. (2001b). The resource-based view of the firm: Ten years after 1991. *Journal of Management*, 21, 625–641.

Batt, R. (2002). Managing customer services: Human resource practices, quit rates, and sales growth. *Academy of Management Journal, 45*, 587–597.

Bauer, T. N., Maertz, C. P., Dolen M. R., Campion, M.A. 1998. A longitudinal assessment of applicant reactions to an employment test. *Journal of Applied Psychology, 83*, 892-903.

Becker, B., & Gerhart, B. (1996). The impact of human resource management on organizational performance: Progress and prospects. *Academy of Management Journal, 39*, 779–801.

Becker, H. S. (1960). Notes on the concept of commitment. *American Journal of Sociology*, 66: 32-40.

Beins, B.C. (2004). *Research methods: A tool for life.* Boston: Pearson Education.

Bergman, T. and Taylor, M.S. 1984. College recruitment: what attracts students to organizations, *Personnel*, 34-46.

Besich, J.(2005). Job embeddedness versus traditional models of voluntary turnover: A test of voluntary turnover prediction. *Doctor of Philosophy (Industrial/Organizational Psychology),* University of North Texas.

Blankertz, L.E., and Robinson, S.E.(1997). Turnover intentions of community mental health workers in psychosocial rehabilitation services. *Community Mental Health Journal*, 33(6).

Boles, Ross, L.E. and Johnson, J.T. (1995). Reducing employee turnover through the use of pre-employment application demographics. *Hospitality Research Journal* **19** 2, pp. 19–2030.

Boudreau JW, Rynes SL. (1985). Role of recruitment in staffing utility analysis. *Journal of Applied Psychology, 70,* 354-366.

Branham, L. (2005). The 7 hidden reasons employees leave. *Sound view Executive Book Summaries. 27*(6),1-8.

Breaugh, J. A. (1981). Relationships between recruiting sources and employee performance, absenteeism, and work attitudes. *Academy of Management Journal,* 24, 142-147.

Breaugh, J. A., & Billings, R. S. (1988). The realistic job preview: five key elements and their importance for research and practice. *Journal of Business and Psychology,* 2: 291-305.

Breaugh, J. A., and Starke, M. (2000). Research on Employee Recruitment: So Many Studies, So Many Remaining Questions. *Journal of Management.* Vol. 26, No. 3, 405-434.

Breaugh, J., and Mann, R. (1984). Recruiting source effects: A test of two alternative explanations. *Journal of Occupational Psychology.* 57,261-267.

Breaugh, J.A. (1992). Recruitment Science and Practice, PWS-Kent., Boston, MA, 1992.

Brill, P L. (1984).The need for an operational definition of burnout. Family and Community Health 6: 12-34.

Brookings, J.B., Bolton, B., Brown, C. E, McEvoy A. (1985). Self-reported job burnout among female human service professionals. *Journal of Occupational Behavior* 6: 143-150.

Buchanan, B. (1974). Building Organizational Commitment: The Socialization of Managers in Work Organizations. Administrative Science Quarterly, 14: 533–46.

Buck, J.M., and Watson, J.L. (2002).Retaining staff employees: The relationship between human resources management strategies and organizational commitment. *Innovative Higher Education, 25*(3), 175-193.

Buckley, W. (1967). Sociology and modern systems theory. Englewood Cliffs, NJ Prentice-Hall.

Buerhaus, P., Donelan, K., Ulrich, B., Kirby, L., Norman, L., & Dittus, R. (2005). Registered nurses' perceptions of nursing. [Electronic version]. *Nursing Economics, 23*(3), 110-118, 143.

Buunk BP and Schaufeli WB. (1993). Burnout: a comparison from social comparison theory. *In Professional Burnout: Recent Developments in Theory and Research*, Schaufeli WB, Maslach C, Marek T (eds). Taylor and Francis: Washington DC.

Byrd, T., Cochran, J., Silverman, I., & Blount, W. (2000). Behind bars: An assessment of the effects of job satisfaction, job-related stress, and anxiety of jail employees inclinations to quit. *Journal of Crime and Criminal Justice, 23*, 69-89.

Cable DM, Turban DB. (2001). Establishing the dimensions, sources and value of job seekers' employer knowledge during recruitment. In Ferris GR (Ed.), *Research in Personnel and Human Resources Management* (Vol. 20, p. 115-163). Greenwich, CT: JAI Press.

Caldwell DS, Dorling E. (1991). Preventing burnout in police organizations. The Police Chief April: 156-159.

Caldwell, D. and O'Reilly, C III. (1985). The impact of information on job choices and turnover. *The Academy of Management Journal*, Vol. 28, No. 4, pp. 934-943.

Cameron, Kim S. and Quinn, Robert E. (1999). *Diagnosing and changing organizational culture*. Massachusetts: Addison Wesley. In Barbara J. Kreisman., Insights Into Employee Retention, Commitment and Motivation (2002). Ph.D. Research/White Paper, Insights Denver 73.

Camp, S. (1994). Assessing the effects of organizational commitment and job satisfaction on turnover: An event history approach. *The Prison Journal, 74,* 279-305.

Campion, M. (1991). Meaning and measurement of turnover: comparison of alternative measures and recommendations for research. *Journal of Applied Psychology, 76,* 2, pp. 199–212.

Campion, M., Palmer, D., and Campion, J. (1997). A review of structure in the selection interview Personnel Psychology50. 3: 655-702.

Campion, M.A., Palmer, D.K., & Campion, J.E. (1998). Structuring Employment Interviews to Improve reliability, validity and users' reactions. Current Directions in Psychological Science, Vol. 7, No. 3 (Jun., 1998), pp. 77-82.

Carlson, K., Connerley, M., and Mecham, R. III. (2002). Recruitment evaluation: the case for assessing the quality of applicants attracted. *Personnel Psychology.* Vol 55, Issue 2, pp. 461-490.

Carpitella, B. (2002). *Recruitment and Orientation 201*. Retrieved on October 14, 2005 from http://www.housingzone.com/article/CA462710.html?text=recruitment+and+integration.

Cascio W. (1991). Costing human resources: the financial impact of behaviour in organizations. *PWS-Kent Publishing Co: Boston*.

Chapman DS, Webster J. (2006). Toward an integrated model of applicant reactions and job choice. *International Journal of Human Resource Management*, 17, 1032-1057.

Cherniss, Cary (1980). *Staff Burnout- Job Stress in the Human Services*, Beverly Hills: Sage Publications.

Cohen, A. (1993a) Age and tenure in relation to organizational commitment: A meta-analysis. *Basic and Applied Social Psychology,* 14(2), 143-159, Lawrence Erlbaum Associates, Inc.

Cohen, A. (1993b). Organizational commitment and turnover: a meta-analysis. *The Academy of Management Journal,* Vol. 36, No. 5, pp. 1140-1157.

Cohen, A. (1995). An examination of the relationships between work commitment and non-work domains. *Human Relations, 48,* 239-263.

Cohen, A. and Gattiker, U.E. (1992). An empirical assessment of organizational commitment using the side-bet Ttsting approach. Relations Industrielles, 47(3): 439–59.

Cohen, A., & Lowenberg, G. (1990). A re-examination of the side-bet theory as applied to organizational commitment: A meta-analysis. *Human Relations, 43,* 1015-1050.

Cohen, A., and Gattiker, U.E. (1994). Rewards and organizational commitment across structural characteristics: A meta-analysis. *Journal of Business & Psychology,* 9(2).

Collen N. Flaherty (2007). The effect of compensation and HR practices on employee attachement. A dissertation submitted to the department of economics and the committee on graduate studies of Stanford University. Ph.D. retrieved from ProQuest.

Collins CJ, Stevens CK. (2002). The relationship between early recruitment related activities and the application decisions of new labor-market entrants: A brand equity approach *to recmitment. Journal of Applied Psychology, 87,* 1121-1133.

Conard, M. A., & Ashworth, S. D. (1986). Recruiting source effectiveness: A meta-analysis and re-examination of two rival hypotheses. Paper presented at the First Annual Meeting of the Society for Industrial and Organizational Psychology, Chicago, IL (April).

Connerley, M. L., Rynes, S.L. (1997). The influence of recruiter characteristics and organizational recruitment support on perceived recruiter effectiveness: views from applicants and recruiters. *Human Relations.* Vol. 50, No.12.

Cook, J. and Wall, T. (1980). New work attitude measures of trust, organizational commitment and personalneed non-fulfilment. *Journal of Occupational Psychology, 53,* 39-5.

Cooper, C. L., Dewe, P. J., & O_Driscoll, M. P. (2001). Organizational stress. *Thousand Oaks,* CA: Sage.

Corcoran, K. J. (1986). Measuring burnout: A reliability and convergent validity study. *Journal of Social Behaviour and Personality, 1,* 107-112.

Cordes, C.L. and Dougherty, T.W. "A Review and an Integration of Research on Job Burnout," Academy of Management Review, 18: 621-656 (1993).

Cotton, J.L & Tuttle, J.M. (1986). Employee turnover: A meta-analysis and review with implications for research. *Academy of Management Review, 11*(1), 55-70.

Cramer, D. (1996). Job satisfaction and organizational continuance commitment: a two-wave panel study. *Journal of Organizational Behavior,17,4,* pp.389-400.

Crewson, P.E. (1997), "Public-Service Motivation: Building Empirical Evidence of Incidence and Effect', Journal of Public Administration Research and Theory, 7: 499-519.

Dale, M. (1999). Successful recruitment and selection a practical guide for managers. Crest Publications. New Delhi. Pg. 57.

Dalton, D.R., Todor, W.D. and Krackhardt D.M. (1982). Turnover overstated: a functional taxonomy. *Academy of Management Review, 7* ,pp. 117–123.

Dean, R. A., & Wanous, J. P. (1984). The effects of realistic job previews on hiring bank tellers. *Journal of Applied Psychology*, 69: 61-68.

Decker, P. J., & Cornelius E. T., III (1979). A note on recruiting sources and job survival rates. *Journal of Applied Psychology*, 64, 463-464.

Delery, J. E. (1998). Issues of fit in strategic human resource management: Implications for research. *Human Resource Management Review*, 8, 289–309.

Delery, J. E., & Doty, D. H. (1996). Modes of theorizing in strategic human resource management: Tests of universalistic, contingency, and configurational performance predictions. Academy of Management Journal, 39, 802–835.

Dess, C.G., & Shaw, J.D. (2001). Voluntary turnover, social capital, and organizational performance. *Academy of Management Review, 26*, 496- 524.

Dibble, S. (1999). Keeping your valuable employees—retention strategies for your organization's most important resource. *John Wiley and Sons. Inc.* New York

Dixon, M.A., Cunningham, G.B., Sagas, M., Turner, B.A. and Kent, A. (2005), "Challenge is key: an investigation of affective organizational commitment in undergraduate interns", Journal of Education for Business, January/February, pp. 172-80.

Dockel, A. (2003).The effect of retention factors on organizational commitment: An investigation of high technology employees. Dissertation. University of Pretoria.

Droege, S.B., & Hoobler, J. (2003). Employee turnover and tacit knowledge diffusion: A network perspective. *Journal of Managerial Issues, 15*(1), 50-59.

Drucker, P.F. (1988). The coming of the new organization. *Harvard Business Review 66*(1).

Druker, J. and White, G. (1995).Misunderstood and undervalued personnel management in construction. Human Resources Management Journal,5,77-91.

Dunham, R.B., Grube, J.A. and Castaneda, M.B. (1994). Organizational commitment: The utility of an integrative definition. *Journal of Applied Psychology, 79*, 370 – 380.

Evans, S. and Kaye,B. (2003). How to retain high-performance employees. Retrieved October 20, 2007 from http://www.careersystemsintl.com

Farris, G. F. (1971).A predictive study of turnover. *Personnel Psychology, 24*, 311-328.

Felsen- Francis, Coward, L.C., Hogan, R.T., Duncan, T.L., Hilkar, R.P., M.A., and Horne, C. (1996). Factors influencing intentions of nursing personnel to leave employment in long-term care settings. *Journal of Applied Gerontology, 15,* 450 – 470.

Fiegenbaum, A., Hart, S. L., & Schendel, D. E. (1996). Strategic reference point theory. Strategic Management Journal, 17, 216–236.

Fields, M.R.A. (2001).*Indispensable employees: How to hire them, how to keep them.* Franklin Lakes, NJ: Career Press.

Firth, H. and Britton, P. (1989). Burnout: absence and turnover amongst british nursing staff. *Journal of Occupational Psychology, 62,* 55-60.

Fishbein, M., Ajzen I. (1975). Belief, attitudes, intention and behavior reading, mass. *Addison-wesley.*

Fisher, C.D., Ilgen, D.R. and Hoyer, W.D. (1979). Source credibility, information favorability, and job offer acceptance. *Academy of Management Journal,* 22, 94–103.

Fitz-enz, Jac. (2000). *The ROI of human capital—Measuring the economic value of employee performance.* New York: American Management Association.

Freeman, R. E. (1984). Strategic management: A stakeholder approach. Boston7 Pitman.

Freeman, R. E. (1985). Managing in turbulent times. In M. Beer, & B. Spector (Eds.), Readings in human resource management (pp. 189–208). New York7 Free Press.

Freeman, R. E., & McVea, J. (2001). A stakeholder approach to strategic management. In M. A. Hitt, R. E. Freeman, & J. S. Harrison (Eds.), The Blackwell handbook of strategic management (pp. 189–208). Malden, MA7 Blackwell.

Freudenberger, H. (1975). The staff burn-out syndrome in alternative institutions. *Psychotherapy: Theory, Research and Practice 12(Spring):* 17-22.

Freudenberger, H. (1980). Burnout: the high cost of high achievement. *New York: Anchor Press-Doubleday.*

Freudenberger, H. J. (1974).Staff burnout. *Journal of Social Issues, 30* 1, 159-165.

Friedlander, F., and Walton, E. (1964) Positive and negative motivations toward work. *Administrative Science Quarterly,* 9, 194-207.

Fundamentals of HRM (2007). Edited by Neil Anderson. Sage Publication. New Delhi.

Gage, Kathleen (2005), "Increase Profits through Employee Retention,"Webdocument:URL:*www.turningpointpresents.com*.

Gaines J, Jermier JM. (1983). Emotional exhaustion in a high-stress organization. *Academy of Management Journal 26*: 567-586.

Gannon, M. J. (1971). Sources of referral and employee turnover. *Journal of Applied Psychology,* 55, 226-228.

Gatewood RD, Gowan MA, Lautenschlager GJ. (1993). Corporate image, recruitment image, and initial job choice decisions. *Academy of Management Journal, 36,* 414-427.

Ghapanchi, A.H. and Aurum, A. (2011). Antecedents to it personnel's intentions to leave: a systematic literature review. *The Journal of Systems and Software,(84)*238-249.

Gillian, A. (1986). Burnout: from metaphor to ideology, *The Canadian Journal of Sociology,* Vol. 11, No. 1, pp.35-55.

Gilliland, S.W. (1983). The perceived fairness of selection systems: an organizational justice perspective. *Academy of Management Review*, Vol. 18, 1993, pp. 694-734.

Giuffre, M. (1981).The therapist and burnout. *The Family 1:* 24-29.

Glen, C. (2006). Key skill retention and motivation: The war for talent still rages and retention is the high ground. *Industrial and Commercial Training,* 38(1), 37-45.

Gmelch, W. H. 1993. Coping with Faculty Stress, Vol. 5. Sage: London.

Gold Y, Roth RA. 1993. Teachers Managing: Stress and Preventing Burnout-The Professional Health Solution. The Falmer Press: London.

Golembiewski, R T and Munzenrider, R F (1988). *Phases of Burnout: Development in Concepts and Applications,* New York: Praeger.

Golembiewski, R T; Boudreau, R A; Sun, B and Luo, H (1998). Estimates of burnout in public agencies: worldwide how many employees have which degree of burnout, and with what consequences? *Public Administration Review,* 58, 59-65.

Graves L. M. (1993). Sources of individual differences in interviewer effectiveness: A model and implications for future research. Journal of Organizational Behavior, 14, 349-370.

Griffeth, R.W., Cohen, D.J., Johnston, M.W., Burton, S., Judge, T.A., Bretz, R.C. Jr. (1992). Careers, *Academy of Management Proceedings.*

Griffeth, R.W., Hom, P.W. and Gaertner, S. (2000). A meta-analysis of antecedents and correlates of employee turnover: update, moderator tests, and research implications for the next millennium. *Journal of Management,* Vol. 26, pp. 463-88.

Guimaraes, T., and Igbaria, M. (1992). Determinants of turnover intentions: comparing IC and IS personnel. *Information Systems Research.* (3:3), pp. 273-303.

Guthrie, J. P. (2001). High-involvement work practices, turnover, and productivity: Evidence from New Zealand. Academy of Management Journal, 44, 180–190.

Haggerty, D. (2002). Five steps to fireproof your hiring process. Web document: URL: *http://www.ideaman.net*.

Hamlet, K. B. (1989). Slowing the service sector's revolving door. Wall Street Journal, p. A-8.

Hanigan, M. (1987). Campus recruiters upgrade their pitch. Personnel Administrator, 32, 55-58.

Harn, T.J. and Thornton, G.C. (1985). Recruiter counselling behaviours and applicant impressions. *Journal of Occupational Psychology*, Vol. 58, 1985, pp. 57-65.

Harris M. M., (1989). The recruitment interview as persuasive communication: Applying the elaboration likelihood model. Paper presented at the Academy of Management Annual Meeting, Washington, DC.

Harris, M., Fink, L. (1987). A field study of applicant reactions to employment opportunities: does the recruiter make a difference? *Personnel Psychology*, 40, 4; ABI/INFORM Global. pg.765.

Hausknecht JP, Day DV, and Thomas SC. (2004). Applicant reactions to selection procedures: An update model and meta-analysis. *Personnel Psychology*, 57, 639-683.

Hellriegel, D., and White, G.E. (1983). Turnover of professionals in public accounting: a comparative analysis. *Personnel Psychology, 26*(5).

Herd, R.; Koen, V., Patnaik, I., Shah, A. (2011), Financial Sector Reform in India: Time for a Second Wave? *OECD Economics Department Working Papers*, No. 879, OECD Publishing.

Herman, Roger E. (1999). *Keeping good people—Strategies for solving the #1 problem facing business today*. Winchester, VA: Oakhill Press.

Herriot, P. (1988). Graduate recruitment: psychological contracts and the balance of power", British Journal of Guidance and Counselling, Vol. 16, pp. 228-41.

Herriot, P. (1989). 'Selection as a social process' in Smith, M. and Robertson, I.T. (Eds), Advances in Assessment and Selection, Wiley, New York, NY.

Herriot, P., & Rothwell, C. (1981). Organizational choice and decision theory: Effects if employer's literature and selection interview. *Journal of Occupational Psychology*, 54, 17-31.

Hinkin, T. and Tracey, J. (2008). Contextual factors and cost profiles associated with employee turnover. *Cornell Hospitality Quarterly*, Vol. 49 No. 1, pp. 12-27.

Hinkin, T., Tracey, J. (2006). Development and use of a web-based tool to measure the costs of employee turnover: preliminary findings. *Cornell Hospitality Report, CHR Reports*, Vol. 6 No. 6.

Hinkin, T.R. and Tracy, B.J. (2000).The cost of turnover: putting a price on the learning curve. *Cornell Hotel and Restaurant Administration Quarterly,* ***41(3),PP.14-21.***

Hinshaw, A.S., Smeltzer, C.H. and Atwood, J.R. (1987). Innovative retention strategies for nursing staff. *Journal of Nursing Administration, 17,* 8 – 16.

Hiring and keeping the best. (2002). Harvard Business School Publishing Corporation. United States of America. Pg.12

Hobfoll SE, Freedy J. (1993). Conservation of resources: a general stress theory applied to burnout. *In Professional Burnout: Recent Developments in Theory and Research,*

Schaufeli WB, Maslach C, Marek T (eds). Taylor and Francis: Washington, DC.

Hobfoll, S. E., & Shirom, A. (2000). Conservation of resources theory: applications to stress and management in the workplace. In R. T. Golembiewski (Ed.), Handbook of organizational behavior (2nd ed., pp. 57–81). New York: Dekker.

Hom, P.W., and Griffeth, R.W. (1991). Structural equation modeling test of a turnover theory: Cross-sectional and longitudinal analysis. *Journal of Applied Psychology, 76*, 350-366.

Hon, P.W. and Griffeth, R.W. (1995), Employee Turnover, South-Western, Cincinnati, OH.

How much does labour turnover cost? A case study of Australian four- and five-star hotels. Michael C.G. Davidson, Nils Timo, and Ying Wang. International Journal of Contemporary Hospitality Management, Vol. 22 No. 4, 2010, pp. 451-466. Emerald Group Publishing Limited

Hrebiniak, Lawrence G., and Joseph Alutto (1972). Personal and role-related factors in the development of organizational commitment. *Administrative Science Quarterly*, 17: 555-572.

Huffcutt, A., Woehr, D. (1999). Further analysis of employment interview validity: A quantitative evaluation of interviewer-related structuring methods. *Journal of Organizational Behaviour*, Vol. 20, No. 4, pp. 549-561.

Hulin, C. L. (1968). Effects of changes in job-satisfaction levels on employee turnover. *Journal of Applied Psychology, 52*, 122-126.

Huselid, M. A., Jackson, S. E., & Schuler, R. S. (1997). Technical and strategic human resource management effectiveness as determinants of firm performance. *Academy of Management Journal, 40,* 171-188.

Hyde, B. G. (1997). Applicant reactions to interview structure. *Dissertation Abstract International.* 59(5) - 2467.

Igbaria, M. and Greenhaus, J.H. (1992).Determinants of MIS employees' turnover intentions: a structural equation model. *Communications of the ACM,* Vol. 35 No. 2, pp. 35-49.

Igbaria, M., McCloskey, D.W. (1996). Career orientations of MIS employees in Taiwan. *ACM SIGCPR Computer Personnel,* 3(24).

IRDA Annual Report, 2012-13

Irving, P., Coleman, D., & Cooper, C. (1997). Further assessments of a three-component model of occupational commitment: Generalizability and differences across occupations. *Journal of Applied Psychology, 82*(3), 444-452.

Jablin, F.M. and McComb, K.B. (1984). The employment screening interview: an organizational assimilation and communication perspective. in Bostrom, R. (Ed.), Communication Yearbook, Vol. 8, Sage, Newbury Park, CA,.

Jackson, S. E., Schwab, R. L., and Schuler, R. S. (1986).Toward an Understanding of the Burnout Phenomenon. *Journal of Applied Psychology, 71,* 630-640.

Jackson, S. E., Turner, J. A., and Brief, A. P. (1987). *Correlates of burnout among public service lawyers. Journal of Occupational Behaviour, 8,* 339-349.

Jayaratne S, Chess WA. (1984). Job satisfaction and burnout in social and work. *In Stress and Burnout in the Human Service Professions,* Farber BA (ed.). Pergamon Press: New York.

Jeffrey M. Buck and John L. Watson (2002). Retaining Staff Employees: The Relationship Between Human Resources Management Strategies and Organizational Commitment Innovative Higher Education, Vol. 26, No. 3.

Jernigan, A. (2008). Relationships and retention: the staff nurse perspective. A dissertation. Texas Women's University, College of Nursing. Denton, Texas.

Jiang, J.J., & Klein, G. (2002). A discrepancy model of information system personnel turnover. *Journal of Management Information Systems, 19*(2), 249-272.

Johnson, J.T., Griffeth, R.W., and Griffin M. (2000).Factors discriminating functional and dysfunctional salesforce turnover. *Journal of Business And Industrial Marketing,* 15(6), 399-415.

Joseph, D., Kok-Yee, N., Koh, C., Ang, S.(2007). Turnover of information technology professionals: a narrative review, meta-analytic structural equation modeling, and model development. *MIS Quarterly, 31*(3), 547–577.

Jurik, N., & Winn, R. (1987). Describing correctional security dropouts and rejects: An individual or organizational profile? *Criminal Justice and Behavior, 24,* 5-25.

Kafry, D., and Pines, A. (1980). Life and work tedium. *Human Relations*, 33, 477–503.

Kahili, S. (1988). Symptoms of professional burnout: A review of the empirical evidence. *Canadian Psychology.* 29. 284-297.

Kaliprasad, M. (2006).The Human Factor II : Creating a High Performance Culture in an Organization. *Cost Engineering:* 48(6),20-34.

Kaplan, R. S., & Norton, D. P. (2001). The strategy-focused organization. Boston7 Harvard Business School Press.

Karsan, R. (2007). Calculating the cost of turnover. *Employment Relations Today,* Vol. 34 No. 1, pp. 33-6.

Karsh, B., Booske, B.C. and Sainfort, F. (2005). Job and organizational determinants of nursing home employee commitment, job satisfaction and intent to turnover. *Ergonomics,* Vol. 48, No. 10, 1260 – 1281.

Kass, S.J., Vodanovich, S.J. and Callender A. (2001). State-trait boredom: relationship to absenteeism, tenure, and job satisfaction. *Journal of Business & Psychology, 16*(2).

Keenan, A. and Wedderburn, A.A.I., 1980. Putting the boot on the other foot: candidates' descriptions of interviewers. *Journal of Occupational Psychology*, Vol. 53, pp. 81-90.

Khanna, S. (2008). Increasing employee retention through employee engagement. *A Challenge For HR Annual Handbook of Human Resource Initiatives.*

Kim, M. and Hunter, J.E. (1983). Relationships among attitudes, behavioural intentions, and behaviour. *Communication Research*, Vol. 20, pp. 331-64.

Kirman, J. P., Farley, J. A. and Geisinger, K. F. (1989). The relationship between recruiting source, applicant quality, and hire performance: An analysis by sex, ethnicity, and age. *Personnel Psychology. 42,* 293-308.

Kirnan, J. P. (1986). The relationship of recruiting source to applicant quality and subsequent new-hire success controlling for ethnicity, sex and age of the applicant. Unpublished doctoral dissertation. New York, NY: Fordham University.

Kirschenbaum, A. and Wesiberg, J. (2002). Employee's turnover intentions and job destination choices. *Journal of Organizational Behavior,* Vol. 23, No. 1 pp. 109-125.

Kirschenbaum, A., and Weisberg, J. (2002). Employee's turnover intentions and job destination choices. *Journal of Organizational Behavior*, Vol. 23, No. 1. pp. 109-125.

Knowles, M. C. (1964). Personal and job factors affecting labour turnover. *Personnel Practice Bulletin,* 20, 25-37.

Koch, J., and Steers, R. (1978). Job attachment, satisfaction, and turnover among public sector employees. *Journal of Vocational Behaviour*, 12: 119-128.

Koeske, G. F, Koeske, R. D. (1993). A preliminary test of a stress-strain-outcome model for reconceptualizing the burnout phenomenon. *Journal of Social Service Research 17*: 107-135.

Koh, W.L., Steers, R.M. and Terborg, J.R. (1995) 'The Effects of Transformational Leadership on Teacher Attitudes and Student Performance in Singapore', Journal of Organizational Behavior, 16: 319–33.

Kohn, L., Dipboye, R. (1998). The Effects of Interview Structure on Recruiting Outcomes. *Journal of Applied Social Psychology,* Vol 28, Issue 9, pp 821–843.

Kristof-Brown, A.L., Zimmerman, R.D. and Johnson, E.C. (2005) Consequences of Individuals' Fit at Work: A metaanalysis of person–job, person–organization, person–group, and person–supervisor fit. Personnel Psychology, 58, 281–342.

Kwon, I.G. and Banks, D.W. (2004).Factors related to the organizational and professional commitment of internal auditors. *Managerial Auditing Journal*, Vol. 19 No. 5, pp. 606-22.

Labatmediene, L., Endriulaitiene', A. and Gustainiene, L. (2007). Individual correlates of organizational commitment and intention to leave the organization. *Baltic Journal of Management.* Vol. 2 No. 2, pp. 196-212.

Lakhani, H. (1988). The effect of pay and retention bonuses on quit rates in the U.S. Army. *Industrial and Labour Relations Review.* 41, 430-438.

Lambert, E. G. (2006). I want to leave: A test of a model of turnover intent among correctional staff. *Applied Psychology in Criminal Justice,* 2(1), 57-83.

Larson. L. (---). Internal auditor job stress and turnover intentions. Abstract.

Lashley, C. and Chaplain, A. (1999), Labour turnover: hidden problem – hidden costs. *The Hospitality Review,* Vol. 1 No. 1, pp. 49-54.

Leder, S. (1999). Hiring and keeping salespeople. Web document: URL: *http://www.furninfo.com/absolutenm/anmviewer.asp?a=3981.*

Lee, R. T. and Ashforth, B.E. (1993).A further examination of managerial burnout: toward an integrated model. *Journal of Organizational Behavior, 14*(1), 3-21.

Lee, R. T., and Ashforth, B. E. (1996). A meta-analytic examination of the correlates of the three dimensions of burnout. *Journal of Applied Psychology* (81:2), pp. 123-133.

Lee, T.W. & Mowday, R.T. (1987). Voluntarily leaving an organization: An empirical investigation of Steers and Mowday's model of turnover. *Academy of Management Journal, 30*(4), 721-743.

Leiter, M P. (1993). Burnout as a developmental process: consideration of models. *In Professional Burnout: Recent*

Developments in Theory and Research, Schaufeli WB, Maslach C, Marek T (Eds). Taylor and Francis: Washington, DC.

Leiter, M. P. (1991).Coping patterns as predictors of burnout: the function of control and escapist coping. *Journal of Occupational Behavior, 12*, 123-144.

Leiter, M. P. and Maslach, C. (1988). The impact of interpersonal environment on burnout and organizational commitment. *Journal of Occupational Behavior, 8*, 297-308.

Leiter, M. P., Clark, D., and Durup, J. (1994). Distinct models of burnout and commitment among men and women in the military. *Journal of Applied Behavioural Science, 30*, 63-82.

Leiter,M. and Maslach, C. (1999). Six areas of work life: A model of the organizational context of burnout. JHHSA.

Leiter,M. and Maslach,C. (1997). The truth about burnout. San Francisco. Jossey- Bass.

Lewis, C., (1985). *Employee Selection.* Hutchison (London and Brookfiled, VT).

Ley, R. (1966). Labour turnover as a function of worker differences, work environment, and authoritarianism of foremen. *Journal of Applied Psychology,* SO, 497-500.

Liden R. C., Parsons C. K. (1986). A field study of job applicant interview perceptions, alternative opportunities, and demographic characteristics. *Personnel Psychology,* 39, 109-122.

Lievens, F. (2007). Employer branding in Belgian army: The importance of instrumental and symbolic beliefs for potential applicants, actual applicants and military employees. *Human Resource Management*, 46, No (1):51-69.

Locke, E.A. (1976). The nature and causes of job satisfaction. In Handbook of *Industrial and Organizational Psychology*. Ed. M.D. Dunnette. Chicago:Rand-McNally.

Lok, P., & Crawford, J. (2001). Antecedents of organizational commitment and the mediating role of job satisfaction. *Journal of Management Psychology, 16,* 594-613.

Louis, M. (1980). Surprise and sense-making: What newcomers experience in entering unfamiliar organizational settings. *Administrative Science Quarterly*, 25: 226-251.

Low, J. and Siesfield, T. (1998). Measures that matter. Ernst & Young, Boston.

Luthans, F., McCaul, H.F. and Dodd, N.G. (1985). Organizational Commitment: A Comparison of Americans, Japanese, and Korean Employees', Academy of Management Journal, 28(1): 213–9.

Lynn, M. (2002), Turnover's relationships with sales, tips and service across restaurants in a chain. *Hospitality Management*, Vol. 21 No. 4, pp. 443-7.

Lynn, M. (2002).Turnover's relationships with sales, tips and service across restaurants in a chain. *Hospitality Management*, Vol. 21 No. 4, pp. 443-7.

MacFadden, R.J. (1980). Stress, support and the front line social worker. *Working Papers on Social Welfare in Canada, No. 1. Toronto: Faculty of Social Work.*

MacHatton, M., Van D, Thomas and Steiner, Robert. (1997). Selection and retention of managers in the us restaurant sector. *International Journal of Contemporary Hospitality Management, 9.4,* pp.155 - 160.

Mak, B. and Sockel, H. (2001). A confirmatory factor analysis of IS employees. *Information and Management,* Vol. 38, Issue 5, pg. 265-276.

March, R. and Mannari, H. (1977). Organizational commitment and turnover: a predictive study. *Administrative Science Quarterly, 22*(4).

Marchiori, D.M. and Henkin, A.B. (2004). Organizational commitment of a health profession faculty: dimensions, correlated and conditions. *Medical Teacher*, Vol. 26 No. 4, pp. 353-8.

Marsh, R., and Mannari, H. (1977). Organizational commitment and turnover: A predictive study. *Administrative Science Quarterly, 22*(4).

Martin, T.N. (1982). Commitment predictors of nursing personnel's intent of leave. *Medical Care, 20*, 1147 –1153.

Mary , L. and Sara, L.(1997).The Influence of recruiter characteristics and organizational recruitment support on perceived recruiter effectiveness: view from applicants and recruiters. *Human relations,* vol.50, No.12.

Maslach, C. (1982). Burnout: The Cost of Caring. *Englewood Cliffs*, NJ: Prentice-Hall.

Maslach, C. and Jackson, S. (1981). The Maslach burnout inventory. *Palo Alto CA: Consulting Psychologists Press.*

Maslach, C. and Jackson, S. E. (1984a).Burnout in organizational settings. *In Applied Social Psychology Annual: Applications in Organizational Settings (5)*, Beverly Hills, CA: Sage, 133-153.

Maslach, C. and Jackson, S. E. (1984b).Patterns of burnout among a national sample of public contact workers. *Journal of Health and Human Resource Administration, 7,* 189-212.

Maslach, C. Leiter, M. P. (2008). Early predictors of job burnout and engagement. *Journal of Applied Psychology,* Vol.93, No.3, 498-512.

Mathieu, J. E., & Zajac, D. (1990). A review and meta-analysis of the antecedents, correlates, and consequences of organizational commitment. *Psychological Bulletin, 108,* 171–194.

Mattox, J. R. & Jinkerson D. L. 2005. Using survival analysis to demonstrate the effects of training on employee retention. *Evaluation and Program Planning.* 28. 423–430.

Maurer, S. D., Howe, V., & Lee, T. W. (1992). Organizational recruiting as marketing management: An interdisciplinary study of engineering graduates. *Personnel Psychology*, 45: 807-833.

McCaul, H.S., Hinsz, V.B. and McCaul, K.D. (1995) 'Assessing Organizational Commitment: An Employee's Global Attitude toward the Organization', Journal of Applied Behavioral Science, 31(1): 80–90.

McMahan (1992) in research paper titled The impact of human resource management practices on turnover, productivity, and corporate financial performance. Mark A. Huselid (1995). The Academy of Management Journal, 38 (1995). The of Management Journal, 38(3): 635-672.

Meier, S T (1983). Toward a theory of burnout. *Human Relations*, 36 (10), 899-910.

Metcalfe, B. and Dick, G. (2000). Is the force still with you? Measuring police commitment. *Journal of Managerial Psychology,* 15,8.

Meyer, J. and Allen, N. (1991). A three-component conceptualization of organizational commitment. *Human Resource Management Review, 1*, 64-98.

Meyer, J. P. and Allen, N. J. (1987). Organizational commitment: Toward a three- component model. Research Bulletin No.

660. The University of Western Ontario, Department of Psychology, London.

Meyer, J. P., &Allen, J. N. (1984). Testing the side bet theory of organizational commitment: Some methodological considerations. *Journal of Applied Psychology 69*, 372-378.

Meyer, J., & Allen, J., & Smith, C. (1993). Commitment to organizations and occupations: Extension and test of a three-component conceptualization. *Journal of Applied Psychology, 78*, 538-551.

Meyer, J., & Allen, N. (1991). A three-component conceptualization of organizational commitment. *Human Resource Management Review, 1*, 64-98.

Meyer, J., & Allen, N. (1997). *Commitment in the workplace*. Thousand Oaks, CA: SAGE Publications.

Meyer, J., Topolnytsky, L., Krajewski, H. and Gellatly I. (2003), *Best Practices: Employee Retention*, Tomson –Carswell, Toronto.

Meyers, D. W. (1992). Human Resource Management. Chicago, EL: commerce Clearing House Inc.

Mianzo, F. A. (2005). An analysis of recruitment research and the implications for human research managers. Downloaded from www.louisville.edu/cbpa/lmc

Michael, C.G. Davidson, Nils Timo, and Ying Wang. (2010). How much does labour turnover cost? A case study of Australian four- and five-star hotels. *International Journal of Contemporary Hospitality Management,* Vol. 22 No. 4, pp. 451-466. Emerald Group Publishing Limited.

Miller, O. J. (1996). *Employee turnover in the public sector*. New York: Garland.

Mintzberg, H. (1978). Patterns in strategy formation. *Management Sciences, 24,* 934–948.

Mitchell, O., MacKenzie, D., Styve, G., & Gover, A. (2000). The impact of individual, organizational, and environmental attributes on voluntary turnover among juvenile correctional staff members. *Justice Quarterly, 17,* 333-357.

Mitchell, T.R., Holtom, B.C., Lee, T.W., Sablynski, C.J., and Erez, M. (2001). Why people stay: Using job embeddedness to predict voluntary turnover. *Academy of Management Journal, 44*(6), 1102-1121.

Mobley, W. (1982). Employee turnover: causes, consequences, and control. Addison- Wesley Publishing Company Inc. Philippines.

Mobley, W., Griffeth, R., Hand, H., and Meglino, B. (1979). Review and conceptual analysis of the employee turnover process. *Psychological Bulletin, 86,* 493-522.

Mobley, W., Horner, H., and Hollinsworth, A.T. (1978). An evaluation of precursors of hospital employee turnover. *Journal of Applied Psychology, 63*(4).

Moore, E. (2000). Why is this happening? A causal attribution approach to work exhaustion consequences. *Academy of Management Review*, 25(2), 335-349.

Moore, J. (2000). One road to turnover: an examination of work exhaustion in technology professionals. *MIS Quarterly,* 24:141-168.

Moser, K. (2005). Recruitment sources and post-hire outcomes: the mediating role of unmet expectations. *International Journal of Sections and Assessment.* Volume 13. No. 3.

Mowday, R. T., Steers, R. M. & Porter, L. W. (1979). The measurement of organizational commitment. *Journal of Vocational Behaviour, 14,* 224-247.

Muchinsky, P. M., & Tuttle, M. L. (1979). Employee turnover: An empirical and methodological assessment. *Journal of Vocational Behaviour*, 14, 43–77.

Muhammad, J. (1990). Relationship of job stress and type-A behavior to employees' job satisfaction, organizational commitment, psychosomatic health problems, and turnover motivation. *Human Relations* 43 (8), pp. 727–738.

Murphy K. R. (1986). When your top choice turns you down: Effect of rejected job offers on the utility of selection tests. Psychological Bulletin, 99, 133-138.

Neilson, G., Martin, K., Powers, E. (2011- originally published in 2008). HBR's 10 Must Reads On Strategy.

Newman, K., Maylor, U., Chansarkar, B. (2002). The nurse satisfaction, service quality and nurse retention chain; implications for management of recruitment and retention. *Journal of Management in Medicine*, Vol.16, No.4, pp. 271-291.

O'Malley, M. N. (2000). *Creating Commitment—How to attract and retain talented employees by building relationships that last.* New York: John Wiley and Sons, Inc.

O'Reilly, C, A. and Chatman, J. (1986). Organizational commitment and psychological attachment: the effects of compliance, identification, and internalization on pro-social behaviour. *Journal of Applied Psychology.* Vol.71, p.492-499.

O'Reilly, C.A., Chatman, J., and Caldwell, D.F. (1991). People and organizational culture: A profile comparison approach to assessing person-organization fit. *Academy of Management Journal*, 34, 487-516.

Omstein, S., & Isabella, L. (1990). Age vs. stage models of career attitudes of women: A partial replication and extension. *Journal of Vocational Behavior, 36,* 1-19.

O'Reilly C .A. III, Caldwell D. F. (1981). The commitment and job tenure of new employees: Some evidence of post decisional justification. *Administration Science Quarterly, 26,* 597-616.

Ornstein, S., Cron, W. L., & Slocum, J. W. (1989). Life stage versus career stage: A comparative test of the theories of Levinson and Super. *Journal of Organizational Behavior, 10,* 117-133.

Osterman, P. (1987). Turnover, employment security, and the performance of the firm. In M.M. Klein, R.N. Block, M. Roomkin, & S.W. Salsburg (eds.), *Human resources and the performance of the firm.* Madison, WI: Industrial Relations Research Association.

Owens, W.A. & Schoenfeldt, L. F. (1979). Toward a classification of persons. Journal of Applied Psychology , 63, 569-607.

Papadopoulou, A., Ineson, E., Williams, D. (1996). The graduate management trainee pre-selection interview candidates' perceptions of the influence of interpersonal and communication factors on the interview outcomes. *Personnel Review.* Vol. 25, Iss. 4, pg. 21.

Parasuraman, S. (1989). Nursing turnover: an integrated model. *Research in Nursing & Health, 12,* 267– 277.

Pathak, S and Tripathi, V. (2010) Sales force Turnover: an exploratory study of the Indian insurance sector. *Management.* 5 (1): 3–19

Philips, J. (1998). Effects on realistic on job previews on multiple organizational outcomes: A meta-analysis. *Academy of Management Journal, 41*(6), 673-690.

Pines A, Keinan, G. (2005). Stress and burnout: The significant difference. *Personality and Individual Differences, 39*, 625–635. Elsevier Ltd.

Pines A. (1993). Burnout: an existential perspective. In *Professional Burnout: Recent Developments in Theory and Research*, Schaufeli WB, Maslach C, Marek T (eds). Taylor and Francis: Washington, DC.

Pines, A. M. (2000). Nurses' burnout: an existential psychodynamic perspective. *Journal of Psychosocial Nursing, 38*(2), 1–9.

Pines, A., Aronson, E. and Kafry, D. (1981). Burnout: from tedium to personal growth. *The Free Press, New York*.

Polyhart RE, Harold CM. (2004). The applicant attribution-reaction theory (AART): an integrative theory of applicant attributional processing. *International Journal of Selection and Assessment*, 12, 84-98.

Porter LW, Crampon WJ, Smith FJ. (1976). Organizational commitment and managerial turnover: A longitudinal study. *Organizational Behaviour and Human Decision Processes, 15*, 87-98.

Porter, L., Steers, R., and Mowday, R., Boulian, P. (1974). Organizational commitment, job satisfaction, and turnover among psychiatric technicians. *Journal of Applied Psychology,* Vol. 59, No. 5, 603-609.

Porter, M. (2011- originally published in 1996) - HBR's 10 Must Reads On Strategy.

Powell G. N. (1984). Effects of job attributes and recruiting practices on applicant decisions: a comparison. *Personnel Psychology,* 37, 721-732.

Powell, G.N., (1991). Applicant reactions to the initial employment interview: exploring theoretical and methodological issues. *Personnel Psychology*, Vol. 44, pp. 67-84.

Premack SL, Wanous JP. (1985). A meta-analysis of realistic job preview experiments. *Journal of Applied Psychology, 70,* 706-719.

Price, J.L. (1977). The study of turnover, Iowa state University press, Ames, IA.

Priyadarshi, Pushpendra (2011). Employer brand image as predictor of employee satisfaction, affective commitment & turnover. *Indian Journal of Industrial Relations*. Shri Ram Centre for Industrial Relations and Human Resources.

PSI. IT Retention: Attracting and Retaining World Class Talent. (2001). New York, NY: Predictive Systems Inc. (PSI). Retrieved July 15, 2002 from the World Wide Web: http://www.predictive.com/pdf/itretention.pdf

Punia and Sharma (2008). Employees' perspective on human resource procurement practices as a retention tool in Indian it sector. VISION - *The Journal of Business Perspective,* I Vol. 12 I No. 4 I.

Quaglieri, P. (1982). A note on variations in recruiting information obtained through different sources. *Journal of Occupational Psychology,* 53-55.

Ralston, S., Brady, R. (1994). The relative influence of interview communication satisfaction on applicants' recruitment interview decisions. *Journal of Business Communication,* Vol. 31, no.1, pp 61-77.

Ravlin, E. C. and C. M. Ritchie. (2006). "Perceived and Actual Organizational Fit: Multiple Influences on *Attitudes." Journal of Managerial Issues* 18 (2): 175-192.

Ray, D. (2003). Thesis, analysis of the theoretical relationships between work exhaustion, job satisfaction, and turnover intention of air force information systems managers. *Department Of The Air Force Air University Air Force Institute Of Technology Afit/Gir/Env,03-15.*

RCI Resource Centre (2001).*Attracting and selecting the best workers*. Retrieved August 30, 2006 from http://www.russellconsultinginc.com/docs/while/hge.html

Reid, G. L. (1972). Job search and the effectiveness of job-finding methods. Industrial and Labor Relations Review, 25, 479-495.

Reilly, R., Brown, B., Blood, M., & Malatesta, C. (1981). The effects of realistic previews: A study and discussion of the literature. Personnel Psychology, 34: 823-834.

Rice, E. (2005). The evolving role of the hr executive. Retrieved April, 9, 2006 from http://www.innovativeemloyeesolutions.com/knowledge/articles_04/article_45_strategic_HR.html

Richmana, A. L., Civiana, J. T., Shannona, L.L., Hillb, E.J., and Brennan, R. T. (2008).The relationship of perceived flexibility, supportive work life policies, and use of formal flexible arrangements and occasional flexibility to employee engagement and expected retention. *Community, Work & Family,*Vol. 11, No. 2, May 2008, 183-197.

Roberson, Q., Collins, C., Oreg., S. (2005). The effects of recruitment message specificity on applicant attraction to organizations. *Journal of Business and Psychology,* Vol. 19, No. 3. pp. 319-339

Robertson, I.T., Iles, P.A., Gratton, L. and Sharpley, D. (1991). The impact of personnel selection and assessment methods on candidates. *Human Relations*, Vol. 44, pp. 963-82.

Robinson, D., Porporino, F., & Simourd, L. (1997). The influence of educational attainment on the attitudes and job performance of correctional officers. *Crime and Delinquency, 43*, 60-77.

Robinson, S., Kraut, M.and Rossouw, D. (1994). Changing obligations and the psychological contract: A longitudinal study. *Academy of Management Journal,* Vol.37, issue.1, p.137-152.

Rogers E. W. (2001). A theoretical look at firm performance in high technology organizations. What does existing theory tells us? *Journal of High Technology Management Research,* Vol. 12, p. 39-61.

Rosen, S. (1986). The theory of equalizing differences in Handbook in Labour Economics, ed. By O. Ashenfelter and R. Layard. Elsevier Science, New York.

Rouse, P.D. (2001). Voluntary turnover related to information technology professionals: A review of rational and instinctual models. *International Journal of Organizational Analysis, 9*(3), 281-290.

Rusbult, C. and Farrell, D. (1983). A longitudinal test of the investment model: The impact on job satisfaction, job commitment, and turnover of variations in rewards, costs, alternatives, and investments. *Journal of Applied Psychology, 68*(3), 429-438.

Rust, R.T., Stewart, G.L, Miller H., and Pielack, D. (1996).The satisfaction retention of frontline employees: A customer satisfaction measurement approach. *International Journal of Service Industry Management, 7*(5), 62-80.

Rynes, S. L. (1980). Individual reactions to organizational recruiting: a review. *Personnel Psychology, 33*, 529-542.

Rynes, S. L. (1988). The employment interview as a recruitment device. *CAHRS Working Paper Series.* Paper 439. http://digitalcommons.ilr.cornell.edu/cahrswp/439.

Rynes, S. L. (1991). Recruitment, job choice, and post-hire consequences: A call for new research directions. In M. D. Dunnette & L. M. Hough (Eds.).*Handbook of industrial and organizational psychology* (Vol. 2, pp. 399–444). Palo Alto, CA: Consulting Psychologists Press.

Rynes, S. L., Miller, H.E. (1983). Recruiter and job influences on candidates for employment. *Journal of Applied Psychology,* 68, 147-154.

Rynes, S., Orlitzky, M., and Bretz, R. Jr. (1997). Experienced hiring versus college recruiting: Practices and emerging trends. *Personnel Psychology.* 50, 2; pg. 309.

Rynes, S.H. (1989). "The employment interview as a recruitment device", in Eder, R.W. and Ferris, G.R. (Eds), The Employment Interview: Theory, Research and Practice, Sage, Newbury Park, CA.

Rynes, S.H. and Barber, A.E. (1990). Applicant attraction strategies: an organizational perspective. *Academy of Management Review,* Vol. 15, pp. 286-310.

Sager, J.K. (1991).The longitudinal assessment of change in sales force turnover. *Journal of the Academy of Marketing Science,* Vol. 19, pp. 25-36.

Saks, A. M., Weisner, W. H., & Summers, R. J. (1994). Effects of job previews on self-selection and job choice. *Journal of Vocational Behaviour,* 44: 297- 316.

Salancik, G.R. (1977). Commitment is too easy! *Organizational Dynamics,* **6**1, pp. 62–71.

Satpathy, I., Das, B., Das, C. (2011). Challenges for Indian banking sector: solution lies in reforming h. r. practices in the sector. *Asia Pacific Journal of Research in Business Management*, Vol. 2, Issue 3.

Saxton, M. J., Phillips. J. S., and Blakeney, R. N. (1991). Antecedents and Consequences of Emotional Exhaustion in the Airline Reservations Service Sector," Human Relations (44), 1991, pp. 583-595.

Sayeed, O. B. (2001). Organizational commitment and conflict- studies in healthy organizational processes. Sage Publications Inc. New Delhi. Pg. 19

Schaufeli, W. and Dierendonck, D. (1993). The Construct Validity of Two Burnout Measures. *Journal of Organizational Behaviour*, Vol. 14, No. 7, pp. 631-647.

Schaufeli, W. B. (1990). Opgebrand: Over de achtergronden van werkstress bij contactuele beroepen het burnout-syndroom (Burnout: about the jobstress in the human services professions- The burnout syndrome) A, d. Donker, Rotterdam.

Schaufeli, W. B., & Enzmann, D. (1998). The burnout companion to study & practice: a critical analysis. London: Taylor and Francis.

Schaufeli,W.B., Maslach, C. and Marek,T.(Eds).(1993). Organizational structure, social support and burnout, in: *Professional Burnout: Recent Developments in Theory and Research*, Taylor & Francis, New York, pp.151-162.

Schein E. (1968). Organizational socialization and the profession of management. *Industrial Management Review*, 9, 1-6.

Schmidt, F. and Rader, M (1999). Exploring the boundary conditions for interview validity: meta-analytic validity findings for a new interview type. *Personnel Psychology*, Vol. 52, Issue 2, pg. 445-464

Schmitt, N. and Coyle, B.W. (1976). Applicant decisions in the employment interview", *Journal of Applied Psychology*, Vol. 61, 1976, pp.184-92.

Schmitt, N., (1976). Social and situational determinants of interview decisions: implications for the employment interview. *Personnel Psychology*, Vol. 29, pp. 79-101.

Schneider, B, (1987). The people make the place. *Personnel Psychology,* 40, 437-453.

Schneider, B. (1976). Staffing organizations. Santa Monica, CA: Goodyear.

Schuler, R. S., & Jackson, S. E. (1987). Linking competitive strategies with human resource management practices. Academy of Management Executive, 1, 207–219.

Schuler, R. S., & Jackson, S. E. (1999). Strategic human resource management. Malden, MA Blackwell.

Schwab, D. P. (1982). People flow subsystems. In P. Bamberger and I. Meshoulam, Human resource strategy: Formulation, implementation, and impact. *Sage Publications, Inc.*

Semler, S. W. (1997). Systematic agreement: A theory of organizational alignment. Human Resource Development Quarterly, 8, 23–40.

Seston, E., Hassell, K., Ferguson, J and Hann, M. (2009). Exploring the relationship between pharmacists' job satisfaction, intention to quit the profession, and actual quitting. *Research in Social and Administrative Pharmacy,* 5, 121–132.

Shahnawaz, M. G., and Jafri, M. H. (2009). Job attitudes as predictor of employee turnover among stayers and leavers/

hoppers. *Journal of Management Research.* Vol.9, No. 3, pp. 159-166.

Sharma, R. (2007). Indian Model of Executive Burnout. *Vikalpa*, Vol 32, No. 2

Sharma, R.R. (2002).Executive burnout: contribution of role related factors. *Indian Journal of Industrial Relations*, Vol. 38, No. 1, pp. 81-95.

Sheldon, M. E. (1971). Investment and involvement as mechanisms producing commitment to the organization. *Administrative Science Quarterly, 16,* 143-150.

Shields, M., Ward, M. (2000). Improving nurse retention in the British national health service: The impact of job satisfaction on intentions to quit. IZA Discussion Paper No. 118

Shields, M.A. and Ward, M.E. (2000). Improving nurse retention in the british national health service: the impact of job satisfaction on intentions to quit. *IZA Discussion* Paper No. 118.

Shirom A. (1989). Burnout in work organizations. *In International Review of Industrial and Organizational Psychology*, Cooper CL, Robertson L (eds). John Wiley and Sons: Chichester.

Singh, P., Finn, D. and Goulet, L. (2004), Gender and job attitudes: a re-examination and extension. *Women in Management Review*, Vol. 19 No. 7, pp. 345-55.

Slaughter, S. and Ang, S. (1996). Employment outsourcing in information systems, *Communications of The ACM,* 39, 7.

Smith, G. P. (2001). *Here Today, Here Tomorrow*, Dearborn Trade Publishing, Chicago.

Smith, R. E. (1986). Toward a cognitive-affective model of athletic burnout. *Journal of Sport Psychology*, 8: 36- 50.

Smither, J.W., Reilly, R.R., Millsap, R.E., Pearlman, K. and Stoffey, R.W., (1993). Applicant reactions to selection procedures. *Personnel Psychology*, Vol. 46, pp. 49-76.

Snell, S. A., Youndt, M. A., and Wright, P. M. (1996). Establishing a framework for research in strategic human resource management: Merging source theory and organizational learning. *Research in Personnel and Human Resources Management, 14, 61-90.*

Society for Human Resource Management. (2001). *Human Resource Practices.* Alexandria, VA.

Somers, M. (1995). A test of the relationship between affective and continuance commitment using non-recursive models. *Journal of Occupational Psychology, 66,* 185-192.

Sommerville, J. (1996). An analysis of recruitment sources and employee turnover in Scottish construction organizations. Construction Management and Economics. 14, 147-154.

Steel RP, Ovalle NK. (1984). A review and meta-analysis of research on the relationship between behavioral intentions and employee turnover. *Journal of Applied Psychology, 69*: 673– 686.

Steers, R. M. (1975). Problems in the measurement of organizational effectiveness. Administrative Science Quarterly, 20, 546–558.

Steers, R. M. (1977). Antecedents and outcomes of organizational commitment. *Administrative Science Quarterly, 22,* 46–56.

Steers, R.M. and Mowday, R.T. (1981). Employee turnover and post-decision accommodation processes. In L. Cummings & B. Staw (Eds.), *Research in organizational behaviour* (Vol. 3, pp. 235-281). Greenwich, CT: JAI Press.

Steers, Richard M. (1977). Antecedents and outcomes of organizational commitment. *Administrative Science Quarterly*, 22: 46-56.

Stevens, John M., Janice M. Beyer, and Harrison M. Trice (1978). Assessing personal, role, and organizational predictors of managerial commitment. *Academy of Management Journal*, 21: 380-396.

Stiff, J. B. (1994). *Persuasive communication.* New York: Guildford Press.

Stout, J. K. and Williams, J. M. (1983). Comparison of two measures of burnout. Psychological Reports, 53, 283-289.

Susskind, A.M., Borchgrevink, C.P., Kacmar, K.M. and Brymer, R.A. (2000). Customer service employees' behavioral intentions and attitudes: an examination. *International Journal of Hospitality Management*, *19,1* pp. 53–77.

Swaroff, P. G., Barclay, L. A., & Bass, A. R. (1985). Recruiting sources: Another look. *Journal of Applied Psychology*, 70, 720-728.

Taylor, M. S., Bergmann, T. J. (1987). Organizational activities and applicants reactions at different stages of the recruitment process. *Personnel Psychology,* 40, 261-285.

Taylor, S. and Schmidt, D. (1983). A process-oriented investigation of recruitment source effectiveness. *Personnel Psychology.* 36.

Tetrick LE, Farkas AJ. (1988). A longitudinal examination of the dimensionality and stability of the Organizational Commitment Ouestionnaire (OCQ). *Educational and Psychological Measurement, 48,*723-735.

Tett, R and Meyer, J. (1993). Job satisfaction, organizational commitment, turnover intention, and turnover: path analyses based on metaanalytic findings. *Personnel Psychology*, 46.

Tewari, A.K. and Tiwari, A. K. (1995) Burnout and total amount of control in two types of banks. Source: Indian Journal of Industrial Relations, Vol. 30, No. 4, pp. 454-460.

Thatcher, J., Bennett, S., Lee, P., and Boyle, R.J.(2002). Turnover of information technology workers: examining empirically the influence of attitudes, job characteristics, and external markets. *Journal Of Management Information Systems,* Vol.19, Issue3.

Thomas, K. M. and Williams, K. L. (1995).The role of burnout on organizational attachment and career mobility. Paper Presented at *Work, Stress and Health '95: Creating Healthier Workplaces,* Washington, DC.

Thomas, K., and Wise, P. (1999). Organizational Attractiveness and Individual Differences: Are Diverse Applicants attracted by different factors? *Journal of Business and Psychology.* 13, 3; pg. 375.

Trice, Harrison M. and Beyer, Janice M. (1993). *The cultures of work organizations.* New Jersey: Prentice Hall.

Trimble, D. (2006). Organizational commitment, job satisfaction, and turnover intention of missionaries. Journal of Psychology and Theology. Vol. 34, No. 4, 349-360.

Tripathy, M.M. (2002). Burnout stress syndrome in managers- a study in a manufacturing industry. *Management and Labour Studies.* Vol. 27, No.2

Tsai, S. P., Bernacki, E.J., and Lucas, L.J. (1989). A longitudinal method of evaluating employee turnover. *Journal Of Business And Psychology,* Vol. 3, No. 4, pp. 465-473.

Tsui A. S. Pearce, J. L., Porter, L. W. & Hite, J. P. (1995). Choice of employee-organization relationship: Influence of external and internal organizational factors in G. R. Ferris (ed)

Research in Personnel and Human Resource Management, Greenwich, CT: JAI Press, p. 117-151.

Turban, D. B. Cable, D. M. (2003). Firm reputation and applicant pool characteristics. *Journal of Organizational Behaviour, 24,* 733—751.

Turban, D. B., & Dougherty, T.W. (1992). Influences of campus recruiting on applicant attraction to firms. *Academy of Management Journal,* 35, 739-765.

Turner, P. *(2009). HR forecasting and planning. Jaico Publishing House. Mumbai. Pg. 5.*

Ullman, J. C. (1966). Employee referrals: prime tool for recruiting workers. *Personnel,* 43(3), 30-35.

Van Vianen, A. (2000). Person-organization fit: The match between newcomers' and recruiters' preferences for organizational culture. *Personnel Psychology, 53,* 113-149.

Vandenberghe, C. Organizational culture, person-organization fit, and turnover: A replication in health care industry. *Journal of Organizational Behavior, 20,* 175-184.

Vash, C. (1980). The burnt-out administrator. *New York: Springer Publishing Co.*

Vault Inc. *Talent War Shifts to Battle for retention*, (2000). Retrieved on March 4, 2006 from http://www.vault.com/nr/newsmain.jsp?nr_page=3&ch_id=402&article_id=5866628&listelement=2&cat_id=1123

Veninga, R L and Spradley, J P (1981). *The Work Stress Connection: How to Cope with the Burnout*? Boston: Little Brown and Company.

Wagner, CM. (2007).Organizational commitment as a predictor variable in nursing turnover research: literature review. *Journal of Advanced Nursing, 60*: 235–247.

Walker, G. (1986). Burnout: From Metaphor to Ideology. The Canadian Journal of Sociology. Vol. 11, No., pp. 35-55

Wallace JE, Brinkerhoff MB. (1991). The measurement of burnout revisited. *Journal of Social Service Research 14*: 125-130.

Wang, J.M., and Kleiner, B.H. (2004). Effective employment screening practices. *Management Research News, 24*(4/5), 99-107.

Wanous, J. P. (1973). Effects of realistic job preview on job acceptance, job attitudes, and job survival. *Journal of Applied Psychology.* 58, 327-332.

Wanous, J. P. (1980). Organization Entry: Recruitment, selection and socialization of newcomers. Reading, Mass: Addision-Wesley.

Wanous, J. P. (1989). Installing a realistic job preview: Ten tough choices. *Personnel Psychology, 42,* 117–134.

Way, S. A. (2002). High performance work systems and intermediate indicators of firm performance within the U.S. small business sector. Journal of Management, 28, 765–785.

Weisberg, J. and Sagie, A. (1999).Teachers' physical, mental, and emotional burnout: impact on intention to quit. *Journal Of Psychology. 133 ,2,* pp.333-339.

Weiss, A. (1980) Job queues and layoffs in labour markets with flexible wages. Journal of Political Economy, 88, 526-538.

Werbel, J. D., & Landau, J. (1996). The effectiveness of different recruitment sources: A mediating variable analysis. Journal of Applied Social Psychology, 26, 1337-1350.

Wernimont, P. F. & Campbell, J. P. (1968). Signs, samples, and criteria.... Journal of Applied Psychology, 52, 372-376.

Whitener, E. and Walz, P. (1993). Exchange theory determinants of affective and continuance commitment and turnover. *Journal of Vocational Behavior,42*, 265-282.

Wiener, Y. (1982). Commitment in organizations: A normative view. *Academy of Management Review,* 7,418-28.

William H. Mobley (1982). Employee turnover: causes, consequences, and control. Addison- Wesley Publishing Company Inc. Philippines.

Williams, C. R., Labig, C. E., and Stone, T. H. (1993). Recruitment sources and posthire outcomes for job applicants and new hires: A test of two hypotheses. *Journal of Applied Psychology*, 78, 163-172.

Wilson, B. and Laschinger, H.K., (1994). Staff nurse perception of job empowerment and organizational commitment. A test of Kanter's theory of structural power in organizations. *Journal of Nursing Administration*, 24, 39 – 47.

Windolf, P. (1986). Recruitment, selection, and internal labour markets in Britain and Germany. *Organization Studies,* 7/3: 235-254.

Winnubst, J. (1993). Organizational structure, social support and burnout, in: W.B. Schaufeli, C. Maslach, T. Marek (Eds.), Professional Burnout: Recent Developments in Theory and Research, Taylor & Francis, New York, pp. 151–162.

Woods R.H. and Macauly , J.F. (1989). Rx for turnover: retention programs that work. *Cornell Hotel and Restaurant Administration Quarterly* **30** 1, pp. 79–90.

Wright, P. M. (1998). HR fit: Does it really matter? Human Resource Planning, 21, 56–57.

Wright, P. M., Dunford, B. B., & Snell, S. A. (2001). Human resources and the resource based view of the firm. Journal of Management, 27, 701–721.

Wright, P. M., McMahan, C. G., & McWilliams, A. (1994). Human resources and sustained competitive advantage: A resource based view perspective. International Journal of Human Resource Management, 5, 201–326.

Yager, F. (2012). The cost of bad hiring decisions runs high. The Dice Resource Center. http://resources.dice.com/report/the-cost-of-bad-hiring-decisions/

Yellen, J. L. (1984) Efficiency wage models of unemployment. American Economic Review, 74, 200-205.

Yousef, D. (2003). Validating the dimensionality of Porter et al.'s measurement of organizational commitment in a non-Western culture setting Int. J. of Human Resource Management 14:6 September 2003 1067–1079

Zottoli, M., and Wanous, J. (2000). Recruitment source research: current status and future directions. *Human Resource Management Review,* Volume 10, Number 4, 2000, pages 353-382

Annexure A – Questionnaire

Dear Sir,

Smt. Swati Pawar- Vispute, is one of my Ph.D. students, working on "Recruitment Strategy and Employee Retention" with special reference to Indian Banking and Insurance sector.

The scope of the study includes private banks, foreign banks and co-operative banks and private and foreign insurance companies operating in India. As your organization is the progressive one, Smt. Swati wishes to include it in the study.

The proposed doctoral research aims to investigate recruitment strategy practiced by the banks and insurance companies and its relation with the retention of their employees. The researcher would consequently attempt to develop a model of cost effective recruitment strategy leading to employee retention. In the first phase researcher will conduct semi-structured interview with HR head on recruitment strategy applied by the organizations. In the second phase survey questionnaire will be administered with the employees of the organization. The questionnaire will be shared with you before it is given to the employees.

You would be provided with complete contact information of the researcher. Complete confidentiality is assured and would be maintained by the researcher. The information shared by you with her will be used only for the academic purpose. I request you to part with the information of recruitment strategy practiced by your organization.

With best regards,

(Dr. M. N. Welling)
Chairperson
Thesis Advisory Committee

Dear Respondent,

I am a doctoral student with of SVKM's Narsee Monjee Institute of Management Studies. As a part of my Ph.D. studies I am undertaking research on "Employee Recruitment and Retention in Indian Banking and Insurance Sector". Effective recruitment methods help organizations to retain employees. I would like to test the same through this questionnaire.

I would like to, thus, extend an invitation to you to participate in this exciting research and share your views to enrich the research work. I would like to have information on the given questionnaire. The data thus collected would be kept confidential and would be used only for academic purpose. Any queries and / or clarifications may also be directed to the undersigned. Please find below questionnaire containing objective questions. Kindly read each question careful and respond to the same.

Thanking you.

Prof. Swati Pawar – Vispute
Doctoral (PhD) Scholar - Management
SVKM's NMIMS University
Handphone 9769 238 773
swati.vispute@nmims.edu.in

1. **Through what source were you recruited in your current organization?**

    - (Check one)
    - Referred by a friend/ relative
    - Rehired in the organization
    - In-house notices / promotion
    - Job advertisements in the newspaper/website/job site
    - Employment agencies
    - Search firms
    - School/ college campus
    - Walk-ins

2. **To what extent the following job facets were presented to you DURING YOUR RECRUITMENT process? (Check one)**

    A. Salary and Benefits offered by organization

    Was the information shared with you? Yes   No

    If yes,

Was the information **realistic**?		Was the information **specific**?		Whether it was **shared on time**?	
Yes	No	Yes	No	Yes	No

    B. Career Paths in the organization

    Was the information shared with you? Yes   No

    If yes,

Was the information **realistic**?		Was the information **specific**?		Whether it was **shared on time**?	
Yes	No	Yes	No	Yes	No

C. Content of Work

   Was the information shared with you? Yes   No

   If yes,

Was the information **realistic?**		Was the information **specific?**		Whether it was **shared on time?**	
Yes	No	Yes	No	Yes	No

D. Working Conditions

   Was the information shared with you? Yes   No

   If yes,

Was the information **realistic?**		Was the information **specific?**		Whether it was **shared on time?**	
Yes	No	Yes	No	Yes	No

E. Co-workers who will be working in your department

   Was the information shared with you? Yes   No

   If yes,

Was the information **realistic?**		Was the information **specific?**		Whether it was **shared on time?**	
Yes	No	Yes	No	Yes	No

F. Level of Responsibility

   Was the information shared with you? Yes   No

   If yes,

Was the information **realistic?**		Was the information **specific?**		Whether it was **shared on time?**	
Yes	No	Yes	No	Yes	No

G. Training and Development

Was the information shared with you? Yes   No

If yes,

Was the information **realistic**?		Was the information **specific**?		Whether it was **shared on time**?	
Yes	No	Yes	No	Yes	No

3. Tell us about the RECRUITMENT EXPERIENCE you had with your organization.

	Strongly disagree	Disagree	Neutral	Agree	Strongly Agree
Communication during recruitment by the organization was trustworthy					
Recruiter showed respect for me as a person and for my accomplishments					
During the interview, the recruiter was interested in learning about me.					
Organization gave me chance to demonstrate my potential during recruitment.					
Organization stressed variety and change in job during recruitment.					
Organization told about careers of others in the company					
Recruiters spoke of job in great detail					
Recruiter had broad knowledge of company, vacancy, and job.					
Organization was willing to answer my questions.					
Organization gave vague and evasive answers to my questions/queries					

Recruiters asked interesting and relevant questions					
Recruitment process was effective and conducted well					
The personnel of the organization were timely in informing me about the updates in the recruitment activities					
I was treated fairly and respectfully by the recruiter during the interview					
The organization had unbiased assessment while recruiting me.					
Did you meet employees who would be your co-workers? Yes No					
On which of the following factors Recruiters shared information before interview: (Check applicable) • Venue • Travel arrangements • Time of visit • Receiving person at the venue					
Organization communicated with me over (Check all applicable) Telephone Mail E-Mail					

4. Tell us about the interviewer

   I had discussion with the interviewer on following topics (Check all applicable)

   • Myself

   • My Strengths and Weaknesses

   • My Job Experience

Attribute	Strongly disagree	Disagree	Neutral	Agree	Strongly Agree
My interviewer was aware of the terms and conditions of the employment					

He/ she had knowledge of the content of the application form					
He/ She was able to control the interview					
He/ she was ready to answer my questions					
He/ she had listened to my points					
He/ she was willing to give me opportunity to present myself effectively					
My interviewer spent enough time with me					

5. What was your view on following aspects of the organization at THE TIME OF RECRUITMENT?

Attribute	Strongly disagree	Disagree	Neutral	Agree	Strongly Agree
The company provides good employee benefits					
The company provides good job security					
The company provides a good career path					
The company has a good reputation					
The company has good growth potential					
The company has a good philosophy of management toward employees					
The company offers good geographical location options					
The company provides good training programmes					
The company provides good starting salary					

6. Rate on a seven point scale

Questions	Strongly disagree - 1	2	3	Neutral – 4	5	6	Strongly agree - 7
I am willing to put in a great deal of effort beyond that normally expected in order to help this organization be successful.							
I talk up this organization to my friends as a great organization to work for.							
I feel very little loyalty to this organization.							
I would accept almost any type of job assignment in order to keep working for this organization.							
I find that my values and the organization's values are very similar.							
I am proud to tell others that I am part of this organization.							
I could just as well be working for a different organization as long as the type of work was similar.							
This organization really inspires the very best in me in the way of job performance.							
It would take very little change in my present circumstances to cause me to leave this organization.							
I am extremely glad that I chose this organization to work for over others I was considering at the time I joined.							
There's not too much to be gained by sticking with this organization indefinitely.							

Often, I find it difficult to agree with this organization's policies on important matters relating to this organization.					
I really care about the fate of this organization.					
For me this is the best of all possible organizations for which to work.					
Deciding to work for this organization was a definite mistake on my part.					

Questions	Not at all 0	Few times a year or less 1	Monthly 2	A few times a month 3	Every week 4	A few times a week 5	Every day 6
I feel emotionally drained from my work.							
I feel used up at the end of the workday.							
I feel fatigued when I get up in the morning and have to face another day on the job.							
Working with people all day is really a strain for me.							
I feel burned out from my work.							
I feel frustrated by my job.							
I feel I am working too hard on my job.							
Working with people directly puts too much stress on me.							

I feel like I am at the end of my rope.								
I can easily understand how my recipients feel about things.								
I deal very effectively with the problems of my recipients.								
I feel I am positively influencing other people's lives through my work.								
I feel very energetic.								
I can easily create a relaxed atmosphere with my recipients.								
I feel exhilarated after working closely with my recipients.								
I have accomplished many worthwhile things in this job.								
In my work, I deal with emotional problems very calmly.								
I feel I treat some recipients as if they were impersonal 'objects'.								
I've become more callous toward people since I took this job.								
I worry that this job is hardening me emotionally.								

	Strongly disagree	Disagree	Neutral	Agree	Strongly Agree
I don't really care what happens to some recipients.					
I feel recipients blame me for some of their problems.					

Questions	Strongly disagree	Disagree	Neutral	Agree	Strongly Agree
I am actively/ passively looking for another job outside my current company					
I would consider leaving for a company that had excellent opportunities.					
I would seriously consider leaving for even a slightly better position elsewhere.					
I would seriously consider leaving my job for a position where I could earn more.					
I would be working in my present organization next year.					

Tell us little about yourself

1. Gender: (Check one)
    - ❏ Male
    - ❏ Female

2. Age: (Check one)
    - ❏ Below 25 yrs
    - ❏ 25-35yrs
    - ❏ 35.1-45 yrs
    - ❏ 45.1-55yrs
    - ❏ 55.1-65yr
    - ❏ 35.1 -45yrs

3. What is the highest educational level you have attained? (Check one)
   - ❏ Bachelor Degree
   - ❏ Master Degree
   - ❏ Professional Degree
   - ❏ Doctoral Degree
   - ❏ Other _____

4. How long have you been employed by your current organization? (Check one)
   - ❏ Less than 12 months
   - ❏ 1 year to 3 years
   - ❏ 3 to 5 years
   - ❏ More than 5 years

5. What is your total experience in banking/ insurance sector? (Check one)
   - ❏ Less than 12 months
   - ❏ 1 year to 3 years
   - ❏ 3 to 5 years
   - ❏ More than 5 years

6. You belong to which of the following management levels in your current organization?
   - ❏ Junior Management level
   - ❏ Middle Management level
   - ❏ Top Management level

7. Name of the organization

   _____

www.ingramcontent.com/pod-product-compliance
Lightning Source LLC
Chambersburg PA
CBHW021402210526
45463CB00001B/201